A Judo Warrior's Journey Around the Globe

世界横行柔道武者修業

Part 2: The United Kingdom

Maeda Mitsuyo

UK 1907~1908

By 前田光世 Maeda Mitsuyo

Edited by 薄田斬雲 Usuda Zanun

Translated by エリック・シャハン Eric Shahan

Copyright © 2023 Eric Michael Shahan
All Rights Reserved
ISBN: 978-1-950959-65-5

Translator's Introduction

The correspondences of Maeda Mitsuyo were compiled into two volumes totaling over 800 pages and published in 1912. The editor of these books Zanun was a childhood friend of Maeda and the two went to the same school in Aomori until Maeda left for Tokyo.

This is a translation of the section from Volume One describing Maeda Mitsuyo's time in the United Kingdom, from February of 1907 until March of 1908.

A Judo Warrior's Journey Around the Globe Volume I	*A Judo Warrior's Journey Around the Globe* Volume II
1. America 2. UK [This Book] 3. Belgium, Spain, Cuba & Mexico	4. Cuba 5. Mexico 6. Return to Cuba & Guatemala

Recent Photograph of Maeda Yondan

世界力士界の覇王 米人フランク・ゴッチの背面。

フランク・ゴッチの正面
在桑港の我が柔道家御藤四段の為め、買はれたり先年、露人ハツケンスミスを破れり。

世界拳闘界の覇王、米人ザツフリー
先年ジョンソンの為に破られたり。

Top:
World Champion Wrestler
The back muscles of American Frank Gotch

Bottom Right:
Front view of Frank Gotch
He currently lives in San Francisco. He was beaten by a compatriot of Maeda's named Itoh Yondan.[1] A few years ago he defeated the Russian Hackenschmidt.

Bottom Left:
World champion boxer the American Jefferies. He was defeated by the black boxer Johnson a few years ago.

---

[1] Itoh Tokugoro 伊藤徳五郎 (?~?)

World Champion of European Wrestling
The man known as the Russian Lion
Georg Karl Julius Hackenschmidt (1878~ 1968)
He refused to duel with Maeda Yondan.
Views from the front and side.

Top:
Western style Sumo, also known as wrestling or catch as catch can. This is how they begin. This is the Russian Lion Hackenschmidt on the right and Obrien on the left.

Bottom:
The Half Nelson joint lock from Western Sumo.
From behind the man has slipped his right arm under his opponent's right arm and grabbed the neck, applying pressure. His left hand has a Hammer-lock on his opponnet's right arm. This is twisting the joint backwards. Using this he will force his opponent's back onto the ground, thereby winning. For more information about this, check the chapter on the Alhambra tournament from around the middle of this book. It discusses the ways the Sumo wrestlers from all over the world fight.

西洋の相撲取組姿

(其一)之はフヱルソン・ザーと云ふ手にて敵の體を覆なすなり。
(Further Nelson)

(其三)右手にてハンマーロツク
の逆手を用ゐ左手にて足首を攻
め敵の體を覆し背を床へ押へ付
るなり。
(Toe hold and Hammerlock)

(其二)右手にてハンマーロツ
クの逆手を用ゐ左手にて脚を捕
へ、矢張り敵の體を覆し背を
床へ押へ付るなり。
(Hammerlock and leg hold)

Images of Western Style Sumo

Top:
Further Nelson – This shows how to control your opponent from above.

Bottom Right:
Your right hand is a applying a hammer lock style joint lock. Your right hand has your opponent in a hammer lock while your left arm is holding his leg. From there you force your opponent's back onto the ground and hold him there.

Bottom Left:
Your right hand has a hammer lock style joint lock on the right arm while your left hand is attacking his right ankle. You then force your opponent's back down onto the ground.

Jimmy Esson   **John Lemm**

Left:
The champion from Scotland Jimmy Esson who stands 6 Shaku 5 Sun tall and weighs 36 Kan. In a duel with Maeda at Alhambra theater, Maeda Yondan was able to throw this man perfectly twice.

Right:
The champion of England John Lemm. Maeda Yondan was able to submit this man with Judo[2]

---

[2] Translator's Note: There are no other pictures in this book. All additional pictures of wrestlers and techniques were included as reference and were not part of the original book.

ERIC SHAHAN

船中の花形

(二) 英 國 (自四十年二月 至四十一年三月)

船中の花形

▲大風波と云ふ程でもなかつたが、船は可なり搖れる。氣分惡くて三日間は食卓に向へなかつた。同室のスコットランド人は大變弱つて、ボーイの運ぶサンドウィッチと果物を食へば直ぐ吐く、其上の方の寢臺に居る前田氏、其臭と音を聞いては、いゝむかついて了つた、小間物屋のお招伴迄した、四日目には少し氣分も直り食卓に向つた、食後サルンに出て見た、其處では船馴れた連中が、カルタ遊びする、ウイスキを飲む、愉快さうにして居る、澤山の船客中、亞細亞人は前田氏一人だ。目に付くので、彼等は徒然な儘、前田氏を取圍いて種々な話を持かける、戰勝國の日本人と聞いて物珍らしく、話題は日露戰談で持切り、此汽船は英米間の定期通ひだから。乘客は八分英國人だ、同盟國と云ふので

Book II
The United Kingdom
November of Meiji 40 through March of Meiji 41 (1907~1908)

Entertainment Aboard the Steamship

While it was hardly stormy, the ship was constantly rolling up and down swells. Due to this, for the first three days Maeda had to stay in his cabin, unable to go to the galley to eat. There was a Scottish man in his room who was particularly susceptible to seasickness. He would occasionally call the bellboy and order sandwiches or fruit. Unfortunately, as soon as he finished eating he threw it all back up. Maeda who had the bunk above him became infuriated by the sound and smell of the man retching. Apparently it was Maeda's duty to endure this man. By the 4th day Maeda was feeling well enough so he could go up to the galley to eat. After eating he decided to go to the saloon, where he found the sorts of well-seasoned travelers who are unaffected by the rolling of the ship. They were playing cards and drinking whiskey and generally having a grand time. Most of the men in this room travelled regularly between the US and the UK, however, among all the guests the only Asian person was Maeda. When they saw Maeda the men all rose in unison, surrounded him and began peppering him with questions.

They were excited for the rare chance to talk to person from the country that was victorious in the recent war, thus for the most part the questions pertains to the Russian Japanese war. Since about 80% of the passengers were from the UK, a country allied with Japan, Maeda felt strangely at ease with these men. And for their part, the English passengers treated Maeda in a friendly manner. So, since meals were held three times a day, the men would order drinks and offer a toast to the sole passenger from an allied country.

This was a great honor and Maeda appreciated it, however, he was also honor bound to purchase a round of drinks for the group of men in return. Since Maeda did not start out with a great deal of funds for this trip, buying a round of drinks was a big impact on his finances. Looking at the men, Maeda understood that they were all young men of wealth. If he continued to spend money in this fashion, he would be broke by the time the ship docked at Liverpool. He would then be left wandering around the dock without any money for the train to London. Since it was impossible for him to avoid seeing the businessman, Maeda decided to spend the rest of his trip in his cabin, feigning illness. It would be a dull time, but he had no other choice.

Suddenly, a thought struck him and he came up with a clever plan. He would hold an arm wrestling competition. So Maeda sat himself down at a table and challenged anyone who wished to seat themselves across from him and arm wrestle.

The other travelers thought this was a fine idea, and soon he had fellows who thought themselves strong jostling each other in line and saying, "See here! I'm going first!" Maeda took all comers but was never defeated. He was crowned the strongest man in the second class steamer saloon.

However, the arm wrestling competition didn't take a lot of time and people began drifting away from it as it concluded, their attention waning. Again, Maeda came up with a clever gambit. "I will stand with my back against this door and anyone that wants to go can push on my throat. If that man is able to make me surrender, I will treat everyone here to a round of drinks. However, if the man isn't able to get me to surrender after one minute, he then has to buy a round of drinks for the whole group! Is anyone one up for it?"

Almost everyone in the room was interested in this new challenge, however, one rather mild mannered fellow objected. "Please stop this violent game! First of all, you may injure your throat and in the worst case scenario you may suffocate and die!" Maeda reasoned with the man by saying, "There is no need to worry! Now, would anyone like to try and press on my throat?" And with that, Maeda removed his collar and stood in front of the door. A young man stepped up, saying, "I'd like to have a try!" The man pushed until his face turned red and contorted like monkey's, but Maeda quietly endured this for one minute. In the end, that challenger couldn't make Maeda submit.

Since he was unable to make Maeda submit, the young man from London had to pay the bar tab for all those watching the spectacle. After that, five or six other fellows stepped forward saying, "I'll give it a try. I'll give it a try!" However, none of them was able to get Maeda to submit. Those watching the spectacle thought this was a fine game and it helped to pass the time on the ship. In the end, Maeda got all the alcohol he could drink.

Just then, another man stepped up. "I bet if I use two hands, I could get you to submit!" Maeda responded. "All right, you can use two hands, but if you can't submit me, you have to buy two rounds of drinks!" The spectators thought this was a grand idea. Of course, from their perspective, no matter who lost this contest, they would get two drinks each. The crowd enthusiastically cheered on the contest. Maeda took in a deep breath and again placed his back against the door. At the signal to begin, the young man began pushing with both hands against Maeda's neck, however, he could tell this was not having the slightest effect on Maeda. He tried switching his hands around again and again, but it was to no avail. So on this day, Maeda was able to offer several rounds of drinks without it affecting his pocketbook. After this entertainment had ended the guests were quite impressed with Maeda. "So who exactly is this Japanese man? How is he able to do that with his throat" They all began chattering with each other. They found when they applied pressure to their own throats, they would cough or tears would come to their eyes. Then one man stepped forward and explained, "Even if five or six of you pushed at the same time, you wouldn't be able to get him to submit. I would say there is no doubt that this Japanese man is a Judoka!"

The man continued, "Once in London, I saw a Japanese Judoka. Hand a pole to two strong lads. He had each of them hold one end and press it across his throat as hard as they could, but he was still able to slip out."

Ude Hishigi, arm break, applied to the opponent's right arm

Instructor's Guide to Judo (Revised Edition) 柔道教範 増訂 1924
Yokoyama Sakujiro 横山作次郎 (1869~1912)
Oshima Eisuke 大島英助 (1865~1937)

Judo in the UK

The other travelers, upon hearing this, immediately surrounded Maeda and began peppering him with questions. "The theory is Judo makes you strong, but what exactly is Judo." The passengers wrapped their arms around him or practiced grabbed him this way and that saying, "What would you do in this situation? What would you do in that situation?" It was all a bit noisy, like flies buzzing around in May. Passengers would grab his arms and squeeze or seize his lapels, all while saying. "I've heard of Judo but never actually seen it done!" They were very curious about this mysterious art, and having a Judo practitioner in their midst had everyone very excited. Among them was a man who had seen a few demonstrations of Judo in London and therefore had a smattering of knowledge. So now that the boredom of an ocean voyage had been interrupted by the revelation there was a Judo practitioner on board, everyone began calling for a demonstration.

So, using his imperfect English, Maeda began to explain. He showed Ude Hishigi and other techniques. Since he didn't have a pole, he said, "We can use this piece of rope instead of a pole" He wrapped it around his neck and had men on either side pull with all their strength. Maeda then showed how he could slip out. Everyone was very impressed and he expertly introduced one technique after another to great applause. He explains "Whether it's juggling or any other skill, if you train according to its underlying principles, anyone can become proficient. In Japan we have abandoned magic and have developed these sublime techniques through scientific research."

So, in the end, Maeda continued demonstrating techniques in the second class saloon until the ship arrived in Liverpool and everyone had an enjoyable time.

When the ship arrived at the dock and everyone began saying their goodbyes, Maeda was besieged by friendly passengers, all vying to hand him their business cards. "Thanks to you, what started as a rather dull journey became an interesting one that I shall not soon forget!" Ohers while shaking his hand said things like, "If you have time, feel free to stop by while you are in London!"

As Maeda disembarked, he had to meet the customs officials. However, unlike when he first arrived in America, the process was extremely simple. In particular, it seemed that Japanese people were given generous treatment. "Are you carrying any alcohol or cigarettes?" the customs officer asked. Maeda answered truthfully that he had two boxes of cigarettes. In response, the officer only said, "Very well." and marked his bags with white chalk as having passed inspection.

Maeda concluded that public morality in the UK had progressed to the point that a typical English gentlemen, like the ones he was disembarking with, were unlikely to be lying, so he was given the same treatment.

Maeda's first impression as he disembarked and walked towards the train station was that both the train station and the interior of the trains seemed quite old and somewhat shabby when compared to those in America. However, the passengers on the trains were much more polite and generally well mannered. The polite and efficient manner of the conductor reminded Maeda of Japan. The train from Liverpool to London took about four hours. He arrived in the afternoon on February eighth of the fortieth year of Meiji, 1907.

Before departing from New York, Maeda had sent a telegram to Ono Sandan, giving his arrival time, however, there was no sign of his friend when he arrived in London. Maeda was just thinking he had not confirmed his plan sufficiently when two other Japanese men walked up beside him. It turned out that Ono had drank too much the night before and was sleeping in. He had ordered the two men to meet Maeda in his stead. The two men said they would lead Maeda to where Ono Sandan was staying.

They discussed what had transpired since their time in New York, as well as the current state of Judo in the United Kingdom. Finally, it was decided that Maeda would stay at the same inn for the time being.

The next day they visited the youth club as well as other Judo clubs run by fellow Japanese in various parts of the city. At this time there were a great number of Judo practitioners in London. Some had been there for as long as seven or eight years.

There was Tani Yukio and Miyake Tarui as well as Kaminishi Teiichi as well as the big man Ono Sandan, who had arrived last year.³ There were also one or two low level practitioners who had started training after moving to the UK. ⁴ Also, up until recently Mr. Nama had also been living in London.⁵ Horikiri Shodan, who had graduated from Keio University and was now researching at Cambridge University was staying dedicated to the path and teaching Judo after his research was done.⁶

Tani, Miyake and their British students had established a very fine Dojo. Further, there were also Dojo run by British showing that Judo was expanding rapidly, however Maeda realized that the Judo community was not unified. Instead, it was instead divided into many factions, each looking to expand its influence. This meant that each school looked at the others as enemies and they would often criticize each other. In short, it was not an ideal situation and seemed

---

[3] Both Maeda Mitsuyo and Ono Sandan (Ono Akitaro) went by "wrestling names" while in the UK. Maeda went by Maida Yamato and Ono went by Daibutsu "Great Buddha." Japanese athletes frequently took names or words familiar to Westerners as a nickname.

"They have had in London a Yukio Tani and a Tarro Myaki, both brilliant exponents of the Japanese style of wrestling ; but Diabutsu, who arrived in England early last month from Japan, claims to be the greatest jiu-jitsu wrestler living. Diabutsu has good credentials, and states that he has beaten Myaki while in his native country. He challenges any living wrestler in the jiu-jitsu style. Should he fail to defeat his opponent inside ten minutes, he will forfeit £ 25, and pay £ 10 for every minute his rival is capable of averting defeat. In the event of Diabutsu being defeated he says he will forfeit £ 1000."

-Morning Bulletin
Wednesday 28 March 1906

[4] Yukio Tani 谷幸雄 (1881 ~ 1950.)
Miyake Taruji 三宅多留次 (c. 1881–1935)
Uyenishi Sadakazu 上西 貞一 (1880–?)
[5] Nanma 南摩 (unknown)
[6] Horikiri Zenbe-e 堀切善兵衛 (1882~ 1946)

like it was in danger of leading to all the locations collapsing. The Dojo run by Tani, Miyake and the British students was along a busy street in London called Oxford street.

The Dojo was well-appointed villa with a wide training area of perhaps 70 or 80 tatami mats. It was quite impressive as around 100 students were taking turns on the mats. While it was wonderful to see so many students, the number of instructors was low. Due to this low number, the instructors were unable to give the students sufficient attention. This was leading to many students drifting away from training.

Suddenly, into this mix of divided schools glaring at each other a highly skilled practitioner had now appeared. The heads of the other schools were nervous and uncertain and felt they were at a critical juncture. However, Maeda was not as they feared, seeking to challenge the heads of the schools public duels and, having won them, use that authority to force all the schools to submit to him. He was seeking to develop his own way. What he hoped to do was work with the other groups to introduce Judo to the world in a grand fashion. He had no intention of uprooting the fields the heads of other Dojo had planted in order to build his own nest in London like a barbarian. Instead, he was thinking of making his own way.

He also thought he would eventually like to make his way to Paris.

Chapter 14
Fights 14,15,16,17 & 18
Newcastle and Glasgow

Two months after Maeda arrived in London, the season when all the universities in the UK compete in athletics events began. He watched the boat race between Oxford and Cambridge universities and found the event was more exciting than he had heard. As if spurned on by the good reception the boat race received, excitement over the other athletics events began to build with all the energy of insects bursting forth after their long winter hibernation. All manner of athletes emerged, ready to test their strength against their fellows.

Maeda decided he wanted to test the waters for himself, so he organized a week long Judo exhibition in Newcastle, the site of all those great shipyards. Since the people in that area were quite familiar with Japanese Judo, the locals were no doubt thinking,

"Another newcomer trying to show off his Judo, I think I'll have a go at him!" because offers to duel came flying in from a great number of young people. Among them was an old Tanuki, a sly old fox, who had previously been in duels with other Judo practitioners. He was of the opinion that, "Judo practitioners can't really put up much of a fight!" and, "I will go to his training session and see what this guy can do. If anything."

Thus the audience not only had an understanding of what Judo was, they were very discerning. Therefore the demonstration and lecture went quite smoothly.

Maeda dueled many men, among them was a man smaller than Maeda, who did Catch-as-catch-can style wrestling. Maeda was able to quickly pin his shoulders to the mats, getting a win in Western style wrestling. After that, he went up against several different men. There were three different types: "small soldiers," men of medium height and tall warriors. Amongst the small soldiers was a champion, a man from Sweden named Neil Olsen, and he was by far the most adept of that group. As far as the big soldiers go, there was a man who had dominated the wrestling world for the past four or five years. He was a Swedish man named Royel. Though he was quite strong, he was not particularly skilled.[7]

This was Maeda's first demonstration in the UK and since the British people were not unfamiliar with Judo, the explanation was not nearly as difficult as it was in places where Judo was wholly unknown. On the contrary, what he needed to do was demonstrate his skill. So when he threw his opponents, he did so without holding back, which greatly surprised the spectators who commented, "This newcomer is an incredibly strong Judoka. I've never seen other Judo practitioners throw like that." Obviously the crowd was greatly impressed.

---

[7] "In Lancashire, where the catch-as-catch-can game, as it is called, originated, all falls count when the shoulders touch the mat to-gether. It makes no difference whether you throw a fellow over your head, and let go of him, or whether you press him down with a hammerlock, or roll him; it is a fall every time the shoulders strike together."

-By Jim Patt of Wigan, Lancashire
Buffalo Courier Sunday, December 29th, 1901

Illustration showing Migi Kumi

Judo: An Illustrated Instructor's Guide 図解柔道教範
Oda Terumichi 小田明道
1941

Part of the reason Maeda could throw them with such ease is that is most of the Judoka relied solely on Hidari Kumi, left grab. Maeda, on the other hand, was an expert at Migi Kumi, right grab. His style threw his opponents off guard and they easily succumbed to Maeda's technique. In the end, they didn't even realize what he had been doing. All because his grip had been different.

His demonstration in Newcastle ended after a week and he boarded the train that would stop first in Edinburgh before arriving in Glasgow, the second largest city in the UK. The people of Glasgow were quite different from those in London. They seemed honest and straightforward. However, their accent was very thick and it was quite impossible for Maeda to understand. This is because they used many Scottish words. It was also a lot colder than London and so when Maeda arrived there was snow piled up all over. The city was famous for sports, and many famous wrestlers in the UK came from this area. There were also several Japanese Judo practitioners in the area, and the city folk were well acquainted with the sport.

Jess Petersen (1878~1946)

When Maeda arrived, one young man after another, put in requests to duel the new Japanese Judoka. Among the big warriors he faced were the wrestling champions Arikis and Monroe. Among the wrestlers of the middle size, Maeda judged a man named Peterson[8] as Ozeki level, referring to the Sumo wrestling rank just below Yokozuna, grand Champion.

When facing the largest men, Maeda found that while they had power, they were completely devoid of technique and therefore easily defeated. Among the midsized men was one named Peterson, who possessed no small amount of skill, as he had previously dueled against Judo practitioners. Therefore, he was as crafty as an old fox. He attacked with one technique after another, really pressuring Maeda. However, his arms and legs weren't moving in unison and he wasn't positioning his feet well before attacking. In fact, he was not moving his feet at all.

Therefore, no matter how well Peterson setup a technique, his initial foot movement was always late which gave Maeda had a chance to reposition his body in that moment. However, despite being mid-sized, the men was still a head taller than Maeda, so Maeda couldn't just throw him like a child.

Maeda figured he could choke his opponent out pretty quickly, so he attacked with that. But when he applied a choke Peterson got angry. Complaining scornfully, "Judoka use chokes!?" So Maeda

---

[8] *The Gazette* – September 26, 1911
"Champion of Champion Wrestlers" Going After Gotch.

La Provence, of the French line, brought to these shores yesterday Jess Pedersen, whose companies describe him as the "champion of the wrestling champions of the world."

…

Pedersen is a German by birth. His home is in Hamburg, and he has a summer house at St. Quentin, France.

…

Pedersen is twenty-eight years old, more than six feet tall and weighs about 220 pounds. He is a Graeco-Roman wrestler, but has been practicing catch-as-catch-can with wrestlers who have been in America. He wears a decoration presented him by President Fallieres of France for saving three persons from drowning at Beret-Zur-Mer, France. He says he has wrestled in 6,000 matches.

switched his strategy and was about to go for a big throw and then shift to an armbar when time was called. In the end, it took him eight or nine minutes to get the man to submit.

It seems the wrestlers in this city were used to Judo practitioners grabbing with Hidari Gumi when dueling, so they were unable to adapt to Maeda's unexpected Migi Gumi. The look on their faces said, "This Judoka was able to easily throw us without using any power. It was really quite expertly done, a very strong man indeed!"

In this city Judo was popular enough that the youth in the city had started a Judo club. The club members were thrilled that Maeda was in town and arrived first thing every morning, practically pushing their way into the venue. Further, as a of show of respect someone sent several bottles of a famous local whiskey to Maeda's hotel room.

Apparently one of the members of the local Judo club was the son of a distiller, so he was able to require several bottles of the highest quality product. Maeda had initially refused the gift, saying, "While I am deeply moved by this show of respect, resisting the temptation to drink them would be quite impossible. So please don't send gifts like this." The man responded with a knowing smile, "For a Judoka whiskey is like medicine. It is used to revive an overly tired body, is it not? Previously we hosted another Judo Sensei. During his week-long stay here we sent him two cases of 720 milliliter bottles and he gulped them all down." He added with a straight face, "Also, we sent him off with half a dozen bottles to help alleviate the boredom of his train ride home."

Maeda laughed at the man's silly story, but he was impressed, someone could drink two dozen bottles of whiskey in a week. "Who was this Judo instructor?" Maeda wondered. "I forgot his name." The Judo club student replied, but he added, "He was definitely bigger than you. According to the other young fellows in the city, not only was this Judoka known for teaching Judo techniques with the smell of alcohol on his breath, when we went out he had us inhale chloroform and ether as well. It hit us all pretty bad and we were a mess after that!"

As the man laughed at his own story Maeda put two and two together and realized that the description perfectly matched that of Ono Sandan.

19th Battle
Submitting the Famous Gangster

The Judo club in Glasgow paid Maeda every courtesy. They took him on a tour of famous sites in the city. He also felt that he seemed popular with the locals.

However, there was an infamous gang in the area, and they had made a five thousand yen bet that one of their members could beat Maeda. This gang was sure of victory because, according to rumor, they were boasting that, "The fight is anything goes, so shove your fingers up his nose, in his eyes. Grab his groin. Anything it takes to make that Japanese guy surrender!"

Upon hearing this, Maeda responded, "So it takes that level of violence to defeat me? If I were to get involved in a bout like that it seems clear that injuries would be likely to occur and it would sully the name of Judo. That is not something five thousand yen would cover. However, the man did apply for a duel in the proper manner, so I am loathe to refuse. Clearly I will have to be vigilant in this bout.

Thus, having prepared himself mentally, Maeda looked into who his opponent was. Upon further investigation he found out that the gangster that was challenging him was one of the most feared men in Glasgow and no one else wanted to face him.

The gangster had "eaten foul smelling rice" four or five times[9] and with that kind of history, no one in the city wanted to face the repercussions of tangling with him. However, since he had applied for a duel by the standard method, Maeda simply accepted the application without reaction as he normally would.

So, at last the day of the duel arrived a burly, tough-looking gangster appeared. He was a wrestler with well-developed muscles and had an attitude that indicated he was going to do whatever it took to win. However, when the match began, Maeda found the gangster was completely lacking in skill. Maeda threw him two or three times and could tell the man had never encountered Judo before. Seeing how awkwardly the gangster was as he rose to his

---

[9] 臭い飯を食う The literal meaning is "to eat foul smelling rice" but it refers to spending time in prison. In this case four or five times.

feet after being thrown only confirmed this. At least for now it seemed as if the gangster wasn't trying to jam his fingers up Maeda's nose or in his eyes or grab his groin. However, it was certainly possible the gangster was feigning weakness as a tactic. In fact, Maeda got an uncomfortable feeling about this opponent, so he decided finishing the duel quickly would be the safest course. Maeda figured going for a choke would end the match quickly, though it might result in a complaint.

Overall Maeda sensed that the man was "wearing a cat"[10] or playing possum. Just then, the gangster went for some kind of amateurish Yoko Sutemi, Side Sacrifice Throw, but this was just to set up an opening to head-butt Maeda. "Ah, this is the man's true nature" Maeda thought.

Though the man was grinning like he was ready to fight for real, Maeda detected a hint of fear in the man. He wasn't making any effort to leap in and attack. Maeda, realizing he had a firm handle on the situation, decided to launch a ferocious series attacks on the gangster. Maeda leapt forward and attacked with his best techniques, and threw the gangster repeatedly using Tsuri Komi, Tai Otoshi and Koshi Nage before falling on top of him and locking him up in an arm bar.

---

[10] 猫被り feigned innocence or naivete; beguiling innocence; wolf in sheep's clothing

Left: Tsurikomi Goshi 釣込腰 "Lifting and Pulling Hip Throw"
An Easy Illustrated Guide to Judo 通俗柔道図解
by Arima Sumitomo 1905
Right: Tai Otoshi 体落 "Body Drop"
Judo: An Illustrated Instructor's Guide 図解柔道教範 1941

However, while the gangster didn't know much about Judo, he knew enough to realize an arm bar was a favorite technique of Judoka to win a match. So, the gangster used his wrestling ability to slip out and scramble away, as fast as a rabbit. Maeda could not underestimate the man, who was a wrestler by profession. Maeda was irritated at having missed his chance to lock up the wrestler's arm. The wrestler seemed intent only on defending so Maeda gradually closed the distance before suddenly seizing the gangster's right sleeve with his left hand, shifting his body against his opponent while grabbing his belt with his right hand. Maeda, having set himself up securely and wary of any tricks from the gangster, he threw with Koshi Nage, Hip Throw.

Jujutsu Koshi Nage by the Judo Research Society 1934

Maeda fell with his body on top of the gangster with enough force to crush his bones to ash. Then, before the gangster could scramble away, Maeda pulled his arm into an armbar. Having finally been put in a painful position, the wrestler tapped out. The total match time was three minutes, and to all those watching it was a clean cut victory for Maeda. Even his opponent, being the head of a gang, couldn't really debate the result and the referee declared Maeda the winner.

Then something curious happened. Peterson, the man Maeda had defeated in a match the other day, charged forward and confronted the wrestler and everyone in the whole place started shouting. The substance of the complaint was that the previous year Peterson had challenged the wrestler to a duel and won, thus there was no way the gangster could call himself "champion." Yet the gangster had called himself "the wrestling champion of the city" when he applied for a duel with Maeda. Peterson was furious at this contradiction and shouted, "You are nothing but a liar! You lost to me yet you have the audacity to call yourself champion?! I've warned you about this before, if you do it again you will regret it!"

After being thoroughly castigated, the wrestler withdrew. It was certainly entertaining to watch a bad guy like this get bounced like a ball, however the fact that it was a local man, Peterson, castigating the ringleader of a gang and basically throwing him out is something that defies belief.

And with that, Maeda had his first victory in Glasgow. Back in the ready room, the members of the Judo club that had paid for Maeda's trip offered a few words of caution. "The leader of that gang is unlikely to let the matter rest. In all likelihood he is going to try and jump you on the way back to your hotel. You need to be careful!"

For Maeda's part, being aware of such things was just part of Musha Shugyo, a warrior's training pilgrimage, so he was prepared for such things. That being said, Maeda thought it best not to get into a fight in public, since locals might get drawn into the scuffle. If Maeda were to throw one of them and cause injury, the injured man or his family might go to his hotel and refuse to leave until he paid for the injured man's medical treatment.

Any newspaper story describing the outcome of such a confrontation would not cast him in a good light. So Maeda relented and said, "Well, I suppose it would be better not to get into a brawl." In the end the Judo club members slipped Maeda out one of the theater's side entrances and escorted him back to his hotel without incident.

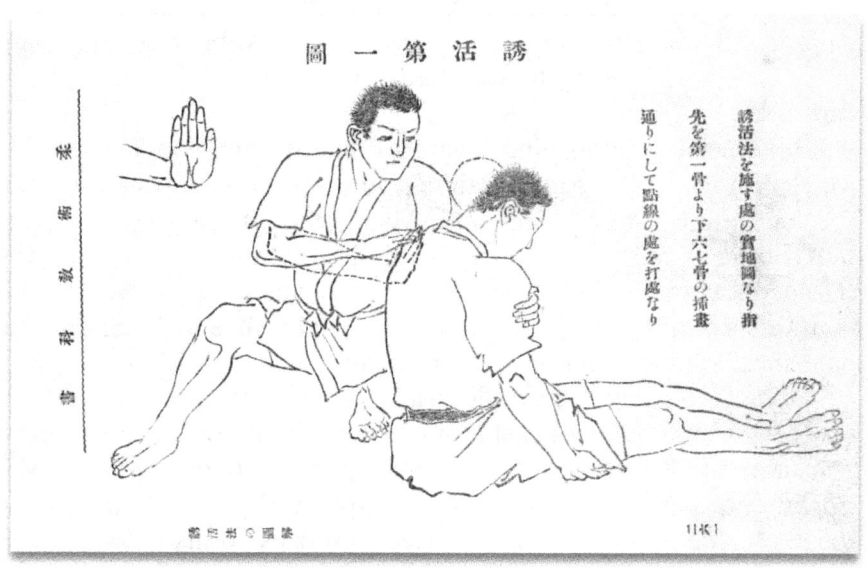

This is Sasoi-Katsu 誘活 "drawing in resuscitation." The point you are aiming for is six or seven bones down from the first vertebrae. The dotted lines show how you should strike.

Randori, Resuscitation and Judo: An Instructor's Guide
乱捕活法柔術教科書
Inoguchi Yoshitame 井口義為 1912

Resuscitation and Fooling Around With Doctors

The next evening there was a rumor that the ringleader of the gang was going to gather a bunch of his crew and cause trouble for Maeda. For his part, Maeda stuck with his schedule as planned, conducting his demonstration and lecture. He decided if the gang showed up, he would deal with them then. However, they never showed up.

Quite the opposite in fact, a doctor who worked for the police department showed up with several of his fellow doctors. Following the demonstration, the men approached Maeda and asked about the Kappo, resuscitation techniques, in Judo.

Maeda replied, "Well, it's easy enough to demonstrate, however there is one small problem. We don't have anyone unconscious to demonstrate on."

So the doctors went over to a group of young lands standing off the side and conferred with them. The youths responded eagerly. Maeda addressed them, "Ok, if one of you guys would just grab this guy's collar like this and choke him until he passes out."

However upon hearing this explanation and realizing what was expected, none of the lads wanted to be the one doing the choking.

Maeda tried to solve the impasse by suggesting an alternative, "This is ridiculous, the one being choked is the one that has the toughest job. All right, no one wants to choke, well then, you guys know how to box right? Just hit this guy really hard with a jab and knock him out."

However, the youth who had volunteered to be rendered unconscious was mortified at this suggestion. "There is no way I can do that! I don't want to be hit like the rubber training ball used in boxing class." With that protestation he turned to walk away. Maeda called out to him, "Wait a minute, I know a way that doesn't hurt at all, and in fact, is extremely pleasant. It is like drifting off into the dream world of the gods." Saying this he grabbed both sides of the youth's collar, put a choke on him until he dropped to the ground.

The doctors then examined the youth volunteer's eyes and checked his pulse at the wrist. "My gosh, he is completely unconscious!" they all declared. Then Maeda administered Katsu, resuscitation and the volunteer immediately returned to his senses. The group of doctors was completely baffled.

The doctors all exchanged amazement after witnessing the youth being revived immediately after Maeda applied Judo resuscitation and one commented, "This is Shinjutsu, an otherworldly technique!" While we clearly knew the man wasn't dead, and we have our own methods to restore breathing to the body, we cannot do so with one quick action."

Maeda replied, "While the West has made a great number of medical advances, Japan developed Sakkatsu no Jutsu, [11] Resuscitation and Killing techniques, hundreds of years ago. That is why Japan is such a great militaristic country today!"

The doctors all listened with great interest. Maeda continued to describe how victims of drownings or people who fell from great heights are treated. "There is a specific type of resuscitation for each of these accidents. Clearly these methods are used when the victim is unconscious. There are also methods for determining if a person is dead or not. In addition, we have methods for re-aligning joints that have been dislocated."

Maeda continued, "From time to time, during Judo training someone may lose consciousness. In that case there is no need for anyone to panic. While the doctors that attend boxing or wrestling matches would begin fumbling about with water or medicines to revive their athletes, Judo practitioners can offer assistance without such things."

Suddenly, Maeda realized who he was talking to and quickly ended his explanation with, "You gentlemen are medical professionals so I don't think you need any explanation of how to restore a person's breathing from me."

Next Maeda went up to one of the doctors and took hold of his arm. Using his fingers, he pressed into one part of the doctor's arm. "As you can see this is painful," he said before switching his grip to the doctor's shoulder. "But gripping here in the same way is not painful at all. I think you can understand the difference. During the course of our training, Judoka become well-versed in physiology. Further, the throwing techniques and joint locks used in Judo are all

---

[11] Sakkatsu no Jutsu 殺活の術 "Killing and Life Giving Techniques" The study of vital points on the body and how they may be used both for causing maximum damage but also reviving a person.

based on and described with concrete scientific principles. Though you all have said that Judo seems almost supernatural, it is simply the result of having learned how to apply scientific and logical techniques over long years of training."

The doctors were very impressed with Maeda's passionate speech and asked, "Exactly how long ago was Judo developed in Japan?"

This presented Maeda with a fantastic opportunity to introduce the full history of Judo. Maeda started off by talking about Nomi no Suke, who lived almost two-thousand years ago, and is said to have started Sumo wrestling.[12]

He then continued by saying, "What we now know as Judo was originally called Jujutsu and was developed four-hundred years ago. However, the man that succeeded in explaining this art in scientific terms is our greatest educator, the revered and respected Kano Jigoro Sensei. Beginning about twenty-five years ago he condensed the techniques from all the various schools of Jujutsu and adapted them. What Kano Sensei crafted was not just a set of techniques, but a way to develop the mind and body."

Throughout this explanation, the doctors frequently nodded their heads and commented approvingly, "It seems an imperial island nation in the far east, with the smallest warriors is set to dominate that whole region."

Maeda continued, "Thinking of Judo as simply a method of physical education is overlooking an important facet it contains. When I was young, I was afflicted by a stomach ailment. I had acid reflux. Nowadays, I am in perfect health, and I could easily drink two bottles of whiskey in a week. Because Judo is a complete system, with a basis in self-defense, it differs from other physical fitness

---

[12] The legendary wrestler Nomi no Sukune 野見宿禰 is said to have lived during the reign of Emperor Suinin (29 BC ~ 70 AD) and is considered to be the man who invented Sumo wrestling. In 23 BC the Emperor instructed Nomi no Sukune to fight Taima no Kehaya 当麻蹴速 whose name means "fast kicker" after Taima boasted that he was the strongest man "under the heavens." Nomi no Sukune fought Taima no Kuyahaya and broke his ribs with one kick and his back with another, killing Taima.

programs. Therefore, Judo training is extremely beneficial in a variety of ways. As you all saw in my demonstration, I was able to easily submit a man much larger than myself. I would recommend encouraging your fellow doctors to investigate Judo as part of your continuing medical studies."

Since the men were all medical professionals, they had no trouble absorbing the details about the physical sciences in Maeda's description and they were overjoyed at the explanation, saying, "Thank you for the very informative lesson!"

Finally, the doctors all talked Maeda into taking a picture with them. Today, this picture hangs in the Glasgow police station. It was a once in a lifetime opportunity to introduce Judo.

After his week-long seminar Maeda left Glasgow and headed for London. On the day of his return, the championship soccer tournament was being held at the Crystal Palace on the outskirts of London. The spectators in attendance were not just from the city but also from the neighboring countryside as well.

The Crystal Palace was a place with large, covered areas and wide gardens for Londoners to stroll in. The buildings were large enough to hold tens of thousands of people. The level of noise created by the spectators at this match, as well as the earlier boat races, was truly astounding. The sound of the frenzied crowd far eclipses the enthusiasm of baseball fans in Japan, yet no mention of the noise was made in the newspaper.

The Judo School on Oxford Street

When Maeda returned to London he spent a few days observing how the old boys from Japan were managing their Dojo. Soon he received an invitation to join them. Since this was Maeda's goal from the beginning, he was delighted to have achieved this easily and agreed. He was then asked to teach a few lessons. However, it turned his friends from Japan were running the Dojo while also engaging in duels at the same time. This had the unfortunate side effect of making the process of splitting profits rather convoluted.

The old boys from the Kodokan had been living overseas for a long time, and it had been hard going. They had started out as student lodgers but were now independent. Unfortunately, they had a haphazard way of handling money, exacerbated by the fact that they didn't all see eye to eye on how to manage the Dojo. While the men fretted over money, the Dojo they had worked so hard to get going was, tragically, headed for insolvency.

"This is what I criticize people in this country about, turning Judo into a product and the practitioners into salesmen. There needs to be greater cooperation. Clearly I need to consider making some conditions for my continued cooperation that will help with both training and the continuation of the Dojo." Maeda reflected.

So, Maeda decided he would initially observe how things were being done and make a proposal that wouldn't result in any misunderstandings.

The Oxford Street Dojo was being run by Tani, Miyake and the British students charged a monthly fee of 4 guineas which is about 2 Yen in Japan. Thus, the students were primarily from the upper classes. Training was conducted in a pure Japanese style, to develop passion and tenacity. There was none of the casual, "I will try Judo out for a month!" that was so common in America. Further, if the skin on a British student's knee or foot ripped and started to bleed, they didn't make a big deal out of it.

In fact, most of the students had been training for about a year with some having trained for three years. There were even a few that were Ko-Otsu level.[13]

Unfortunately, due to the large number of students, there were not enough Sensei to go around. Since the British students were all big and hard to physically manipulate, the senior students were often called forward to act as assistants. The senior students included the students ranked Ko-Otsu level, who were somewhat reluctant to act as assistant instructors. Since Judo is an art unique to Japan, many felt it was strange not to be taught by a Japanese person.

Thus part of the reason for student attrition before Maeda arrived, was dissatisfaction with this way of running the Dojo.

However, when students heard that a man of Maeda's reputation

---

[13] Ko-Otsu 甲乙 This refers to the grading system used before the Kyu, colored belt system. There were three ranks Ko, Otsu, Hei 甲乙丙 before Shodan, first degree black belt. Historically, these Kanji were often used to rank people and things similar to A, B, C.

was coming to teach, they were almost ill with joy. Even former students who had stopped training began to filter back into the Dojo.

Maeda felt the students were quite unlike the Americans who though they could learn the Gokui, the ultimate secrets, of the art of Judo in a month. On the other hand the English students studied with tenacity and drive. This in turn inspired Maeda who threw himself wholeheartedly into training. He did his best to explain with his incomplete language ability. The students asked about things they didn't understand and Maeda taught them techniques they hadn't been introduced to. Overall the students were overjoyed with Maeda's way of teaching. To be sure the instruction the English students had received up to that point was in no way incorrect, it is just that there are techniques people are good at and techniques they are not so good at. What Maeda was able to do was supplement the teaching done thus far with his own particular set of skills, and was able to help them to cover gaps in their knowledge.

As it turned out, if Maeda did not show up at the Dojo, the students were almost comically sad. The students that had been training for three years of more would in fact call first and confirm that Maeda would be teaching. "Will Maeda Sensei be there today?" and other such calls were not uncommon. Frequently what would happen is only after hearing, "He is already here." Or "He is scheduled to teach today" would they head to the Dojo. In short, Maeda was carrying the whole Dojo.

After two or three months, Maeda was familiar with most of the students and they had become more like acquaintances than students in many cases. Next, Maeda decided to go to the women's training sessions. Maeda heard that the women complained a lot so initially he stayed on the sidelines.

However eventually he decided to teach a class. The women were able to discern that Maeda had real ability and from then on requested lessons from "Mr. Maeda." While teaching this class there were more than a few opportunities for him to be depraved, however Maeda never once "got his hands wet." Among the students there were two or three women and men that were from the royal family. This Judo Dojo, if you could call it that, was really more of a Judo-Academy, which also had branches in the Portsmouth naval yard and Cambridge University. Previously an instructor from the London Dojo had been sent to the military base, however in this case, the instructor had previously been a sailor on a coal transport barge. After retiring from sailing, he had trained Judo for a short time in London before being promoted to instructor. So clearly the breadth of his technique was not sufficient to be a Judo Sensei. The school for their part had kept him on for a semester but declined to retain him for the following semester.

While this was going on, the highly skilled Tani and Miyake and Ono Sandan were all busy engaging in public duels while simultaneously teaching at the school to make a little money. They were sweating dawn to dusk every day it was an impossible pace to maintain, thus the fact that membership in the Judo Academy was declining was not unexpected. The Judo Academy was located on Oxford Street a place equivalent to the Ginza shopping area of Tokyo. The combination of rent water and electric bills added up to ¥1000 a month period add to that the instructors' monthly salaries, a secretary as well as general expenses and the finances of the school were teetering on the brink.

If the Judo instructors all cooperated and focused on teaching at the school, while using their free time for duels, the number of students would no doubt increase. This would make the branch schools a viable prospect, which would help ensure the school continued successfully. However, the focus of the Judo Sensei at the school was dueling and they left the day-to-day instruction in the hands of the less than qualified assistants thus the number of students was steadily declining.

Apparently at one point, when the school was at its peak, someone had offered the equivalent of 20,000 yen for the school. However since the school was managed by an amalgamation of Japanese and English they had to refuse the offer as the situation was too complicated and an agreement between all partners couldn't be made.

For their part the Japanese position was, "We've gone to a lot of trouble to set this Dojo up, it would be a shame to sell it to another person." Now though they realized they should have sold it when they had the chance.

After that offer, the economics of maintaining the Dojo became more and more difficult. Part of the reason is that they started running it like a company. At one point, there was a certain British man running it and he was very effective, however he moved to

Canada on business and he left the management to a friend of his.

The new owner would, without fail, slip the weekly allotment of funds into his pocket. He considered the school as a way to enrich himself and he worked for himself, not for the school or for Judo. When money began to get tight, he simply slipped the money for rent and electricity into his pocket and didn't pay the bills.

Maeda's suggestion to protect the accumulation of further debt was to close the Oxford Street Dojo and move to a cheaper location. However, even for this plan, there weren't enough remaining funds to pay off their debts at the current location and move to another period some of the British students also made an offer, "If Maeda Sensei agrees to be the head teacher then we will provide the funds necessary to pay off the debts here and move to another location."

Maeda decided he did not want to get in the middle of this situation. He had joined the Oxford Dojo to train Judo and to have a little fun at the same time. While helping out with the teaching was fine, people would be critical of him if he half-heartedly inserted himself into the situation and did some backroom deal to take over the business. Maeda wanted to avoid the invariable rumors that would start once word money was changing hands began. In addition Maeda had another offer from a man involved in the running of the Oxford Dojo. The man had inquired as to whether or not Maeda would interested in conducting a week long private lesson. Maeda considered the offer of a week's pay but said, "For the time being I would like to focus my energies on keeping the Oxford St. Judo Academy open. Right now my focus is on preserving this school and promoting Judo."

Having committed himself to getting the Judo Academy in order, Maeda talked the old boys from the Kodokan and asked them to try and get money from their friends. Once this was achieved, he immediately use that money to pay off the overdue rent. Thus the Japanese Judo Academy in London, a place that had once flourished on a street equivalent to Ginza in Tokyo, was finally closed. To Maeda it seemed as if he had arrived in-country only to officiate the last rites.

This was around the middle of July, and the temperature was very high. Most of the upper-class people had fled to summer getaways by the shore to escape the heat, so it seemed as if all of London was taking a break. Thus for now the plan was to wait until summer turned to fall and the weather began to cool, so the group of Judoka could set about trying to find a building to use so they could restart the Judo Academy as soon as possible.

During the summer Maeda had no plans, however one of the members of the Judo Academy, who had become a good friend, asked Maeda to come to his summer house once or twice a week to teach Judo. Quite by chance he had another offer to teach Gekken and Judo. Therefore, Maeda decided to spend the summer in London and he took a steam locomotive out to the summer residence where he taught Judo. The trip took an hour and a half each way.

Worth More than a Sukesada Sword

One of the men who hired Maeda for the summer was a student at Oxford University who also trained at the Judo Academy. Though he was a young man he lived in a house in the country and was renting a room while in London. He had calculated the time Maeda would arrive at the station and drove out to meet him in an automobile. Arriving at the house he met the young man's father who was also quite a sportsman. The mother as well as a younger sister appeared and Maeda suggested teaching Judo to the whole family. They were overjoyed at this proposal and accepted.

On sunny days it was too hot to train on the carpets spread on the floor, so they went outside and trained on the lawn out back. Recently Western education had been experimenting with outside schools, and indeed training in the summer fields felt grand. Everyone could breathe fresh air.

Once outside Maeda realized since the space was much larger than the typical 20 to 30 mat size of a Judo Dojo, everyone could roll in any direction without fear. Maeda learned that the father was a wealthy businessman who owned a large soup manufacturing company. Thus, he could afford a stable of twenty horses at his country house and had four or five automobiles along with their residence which was more like a castle than a house. The interior of was well appointed with lavish decorations.

Maeda was travelling out to this lad's house three times a week for training, however, the student and his family had decided to travel to France for a month, so that training ended.

The other student who hired Maeda for private lessons was also quite wealthy and owned multiple automobiles.[14] He loved Japan and had his house decorated with Katana and other weapons as well as pieces of Samurai Armor. In particular, he was fond of archery and had bows from Japan, China, India and various other counties on display. An avid shooter, he could hit the bull's eye with an arrow ninety-nine out of a hundred times. The lad declared, "Indian bows are the best!"

Since this lad was so fond of archery he had devoted an entire room on the second floor of his house to the maintenance of his equipment. He enjoyed repairing his archery equipment as one aspect of his training.

The lad also owned a Wakizashi made by the famous swordsmith Sukesada on display.[15] This fine piece he bought for fifty yen from an antiques dealer in Japan. He also wanted to train Judo and Gekken three times a week.

---

[14] These students are kept fairly ambiguous, so it is hard to differentiate between them.

[15] "From the Kamakura Period, the town of Osafune in Bizen Province (today the eastern portion of Okayama Prefecture) prospered by sword production with its group of leading swordsmiths. There the group established the renowned school of Osafune or Bizen, named after the location, which was followed for the succeeding centuries. In the late years of the Muromachi Period there were nearly one hundred swordsmiths in Osafune who produced many excellent pieces of blades for the samurai class. Sukesada was most singular among them. Thus many swordsmiths and their descendants took after and called themselves "Sukesada". In some respect "Sukesada" was accepted as a brand name."

-Ryuchi Moriguchi
Head Curator, Osaka Municipal Museum, 1986

Maeda had done Gekken while in junior high school so he knew the fundamentals of how to hold the Shinai, bamboo training sword, as well as how to strike.[16] However Maeda had not really trained since the demonstration at the summer retreat in Boston. Initially, Maeda tried to train with the calm professionalism of a sword Sensei, however the lad was big even by English standards and quite strong. If Maeda missed a block and got hit, it felt like his head was going to split in two. The impact left his ears ringing like someone had struck a great bell. By the end of the first month "Gekken Sensei Maeda" had had quite a few close calls.

One day after training, the subject turned to Nihonto, Japanese swords. The lad said, "I've heard that Japanese swords are remarkably sharp, however I have never tried cutting with one, so I am not entirely convinced. Today I would like to test out just how sharp that Wakizashi made by Sukesada is." He added, "I also have two or three cheap swords that I would like to try cutting with first." The lad then produced a length of pipe used for gas lines. It was made of lead and about 8 Sun, 24 cm/ 9 in, in circumference. Maeda first picked up one of the cheap swords and went into Dai Jodan, upper stance, with the sword high above his head. He cut down but the sword went less than half-way through the pipe before snapping with a sharp *Ping!* sound. The second of the cheap swords cut less than a third of the way through the lead pipe before bending into the shape of an archer's bow. While it could certainly be said skill plays a role in test cutting, and Maeda was no expert, but the first two swords were clearly inferior.

Finally, the lad cut with the Sukesada sword. The blade cut the pipe cleanly in half and there wasn't a mark on the blade. Next, Maeda took up the Sukesada and cut with the same spectacular result. The lad was overjoyed, and praised Japanese swords, "If you cut two or three times with a sword from other countries, the blades are basically worthless after that!"

---

[16] Gekken 撃剣 a proto-kendo martial art developed in the Edo Era when dueling was banned. Combatants typically wore bamboo armor and used first wooden swords and later bamboo swords. Combatants could use kicks, strikes, foot sweeps and tackle opponents to the ground.

"Humans are not exactly as tough as those gas pipes." Maeda noted. "That's alright," the lad replied, "Humans tend to cut through more coins than a Sukesada!" and gave a great laugh.
Clearly the fellow had a jovial disposition.

Fight 20
Cutting a Swath Through the Cambridge Students

Eventually summer ended and Maeda received a letter from the Oxford University student that had gone to Paris with his family. It said, "I've just returned, are you willing to travel out to our country villa?"

So, Maeda caught the train out to the villa. The lad was overjoyed when Maeda arrived. "It has only been a month since we last met but it feels like it's been a year. The villa in Paris was frightfully dull! My arms have been aching to do Judo! So much so that I convinced my family to return early!" The lad was not trying to flatter Maeda, he was genuinely passionate about Judo.

The weather was cloudy on the day Maeda arrived so training outside would not be pleasant, therefore they began training inside. At some point the student's mother and younger sister appeared. Maeda was shocked to see that both of them had their heads and arms wrapped in bandages.

"What on earth happened to you?!" Maeda exclaimed, baffled. With tears welling in his eyes, the boy explained. "We went on a car trip to see the countryside around Paris. Unfortunately, the driver lost control and the car flipped. As you can see, my mother and sister were injured."

Since the lad's mother was a full-grown woman in middle age, some damage to her face would not adversely affect her life, the younger sister was another matter. The girl was only thirteen or fourteen years old and she had injuries on her face. Maeda's heart broke thinking of how she was likely going to have to abandon finding a sweetheart for the time being.[17]

The student continued the story, "I was riding in the car as well, but when the car flipped, I was thrown out of the car. When I hit the ground I rolled by habit, just like we have been doing every day in

---

[17] Maeda uses the English word "Sweetheart."

Judo practice, therefore I was completely uninjured. Clearly, the fact that I was uninjured in the car crash is all due to Judo. As proof, the driver I was sitting beside was severely injured and is still in the hospital in Paris, and will probably end up dying."

While Maeda was adamantly against making a situation fit his needs, this story clearly showed that Judo training can help you to escape unscathed from dangerous situations. This served to energize Maeda and he threw himself into training, which also inspired the lad he was training who commented, "I want to spend as much time as possible training Judo, and I am also going to try and get one of my friends involved."

So, in the time before university classes started, Maeda began teaching the lad and his friend three times a week. The friend was a giant who towered over Maeda, however he was a bit clumsy so teaching him was difficult at first. Not only was he extremely tall he was also very strong, and he had a tendency to rely on his strength instead of technique. The other university student was the same and it was clear they had developed some bad habits. Maeda cautioned them about this, but it proved a difficult habit to correct. However, by the time university classes were set to begin the pair had improved somewhat.

Though the taller of the students returned to Oxford, he frequently sent letters to Maeda, one of which was an invitation. "A school Judo class is forming, will you come and teach?" However Maeda was focused on restarting the Judo Academy. Fortunately, a graduate of Keio University, Fujizaki Tachimaro Sandan was attending Oxford, so Maeda wrote a letter to him introducing the student. Shortly thereafter he received word that a class had formed and that training was progressing.

As for the other student who was training both Judo and Gekken, Maeda continued his private lessons. At one point an invitation arrived from a Japanese exchange student from Keio University, who was studying at Oxford named Horikiri Nidan.[18] He wanted Maeda's help with a Judo demonstration. Horikiri Nidan's plan was to demonstrate the Kodokan Nage no Kata, Throwing Sequence, and then show Randori, free sparring.

---

[18] Horikiri Zenbe-e 堀切善兵衛 (1882~ 1946)

Translator's Note:

The Nage no Kata, Throwing Sequence, was developed by Kano Jigoro to illustrate principles of.
The sequence is composed of three techniques from each of the five throwing methods in Judo:

1. Te-waza 手技 – Hand Techniques
2. Koshi-waza 腰技 – Hip Techniques
3. Ashi-waza 足技 – Foot Techniques
4. Ma-sutemi-waza 真捨身技 – True Sacrifice Techniques
5. Yoko-sutemi-waza 横捨身技 – Side Sacrifice Techniques

Each of the following fifteen techniques are performed twice, once on the right side and once on the left. The following illustrations are all from:

The Essence of Practical Judo for Students
最も実際的な学生柔道の粋
By Watanabe Tadashi 渡部正 & Takanezawa Kohi 高根沢光位
1926

Both combatants approach each other and take hold of each other in Migi Shizentai, Right Natural Stance.

将に受手を引き倒さうとするところ.

Uki Otoshi – Floating Drop 1
This shows the moment you are about to topple your opponent.

受手を投げたる場合の両人の位置.

Uki Otoshi – Floating Drop 2
This shows how your bodies should be positioned after the throw.

Seoi Nage – Shoulder Throw 1~3
Clockwise from top left: Step forward with your right foot and block your opponent's strike with your left hand. Then ready to throw with Seoi Nage. The final picture shows after the throw.

・擔ぎ上げに將の手受を擔ぎ上げんとするところ

・擔ぎ上げに將て投げんとするところ

・受手を投げたるの場合の兩人の位置

Kata Guruma – Shoulder Wheel 1~3
Clockwise from top left: You have already loaded the opponent on your shoulders. The next illustration shows after you have lifted him up and are readying to throw. Finally the position after the throw.

Uki Goshi – Floating Hip 1~2
Top: You are set up to throw your opponent.
Bottom: This shows how by twisting your hips you can throw your opponent.

Uki Goshi – Floating Hip Throw 3
This shows how both combatants should be positioned after the throw.

Harai Goshi – Sweeping Hip Throw 1~2
Top: You have pulled your opponent's body against your own.
Bottom: This shows the moment you throw after sweeping the opponent off balance with your hip.

Harai Goshi – Sweeping Hip Throw 3
Top: How both combatants should be positioned after the throw.

Tsuri Komi Goshi – Lifting Hip Throw 1 ~ 4
Clockwise from top left: On your third step, slip your hip against your opponent. Drop your hips. Extend your chest forward and throw. After the throw, both combatants should be positioned as

shown.

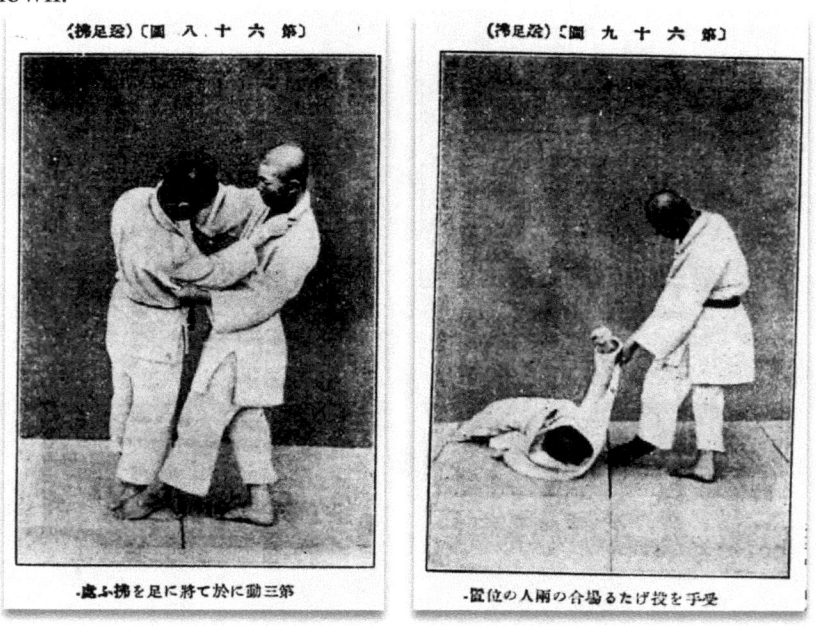

Okuri Ashi Barai – Outward Foot Sweep 1 ~ 2
Left: On your third step, sweep your opponent's foot.
Right: After the throw, both combatants should be positioned as shown.

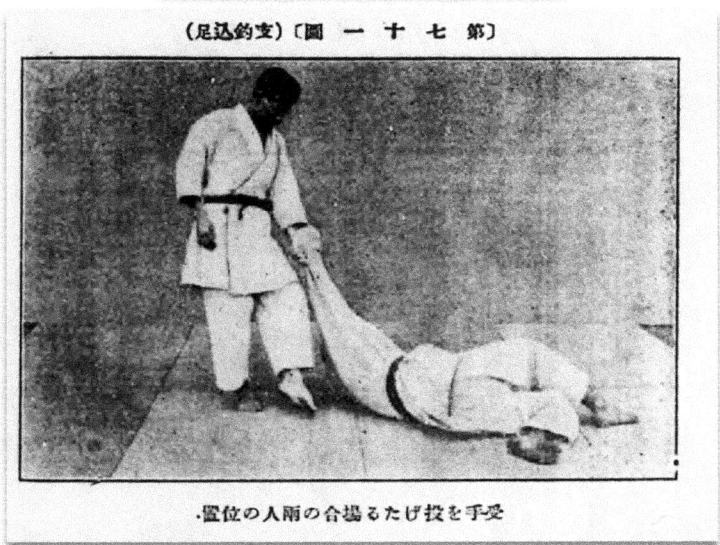

Sasae Tsurikomi Ashi – Supporting Lift-Pull Throw 1 ~ 2
Top: This shows how you have blocked your opponent's right foot and are readying to throw.
Bottom: After the throw, both combatants should be positioned as shown.

Uchi Mata – Inner Thigh Throw 1 ~ 3
Clockwise from top left: You are readying to raise your thigh and throw. This shows your positioning as your leg is raised to throw. After the throw, both combatants should be positioned as shown.

Tomoe Nage – Spiral Throw 1 ~ 3
Clockwise from top left: To set up for Tomoe Nage, plant your right foot between your opponent's feet. The moment you throw. After the throw, both combatants should be positioned as shown.

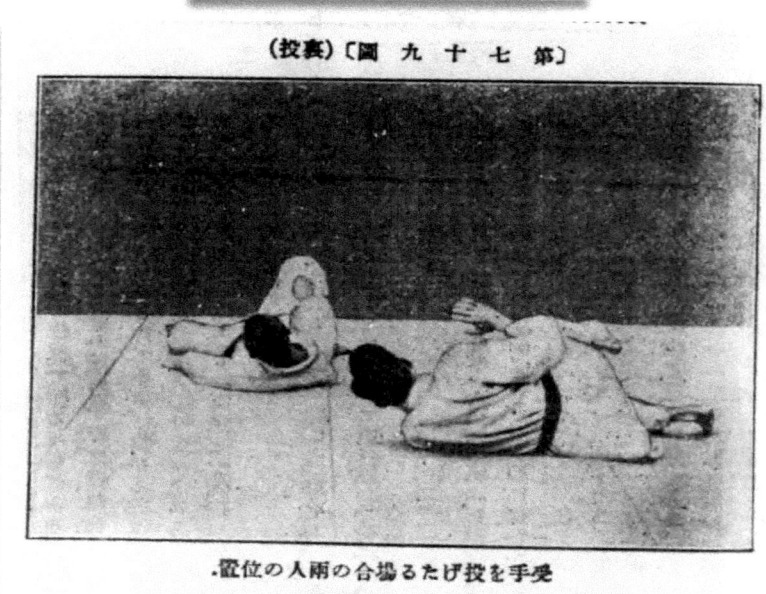

Ura Nage – Reverse Throw 1 ~ 2
Top: The opponent tries to strike you. Respond by blocking his punch and wrapping him up. Bottom: After the throw, both combatants should be positioned as shown.

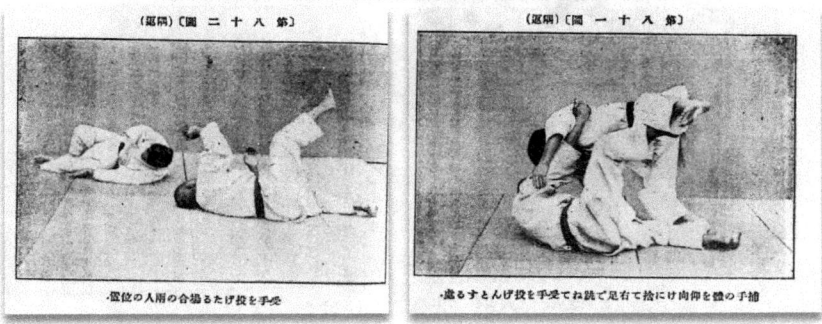

Tomoe Nage – Spiral Throw 1 ~ 3
Clockwise from top left: To set up for Tomoe Nage, plant your right foot between your opponent's feet. The moment you throw. After the throw, both combatants should be positioned as shown.

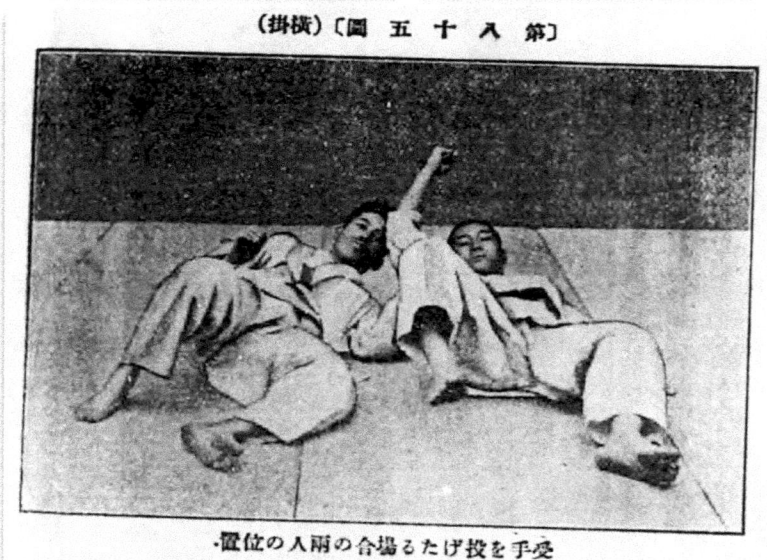

Yoko Kake – Side Hook 1 ~ 3
Clockwise from top left: Set up the technique by forcing your opponent's body perpendicular to you. As you sweep his foot drop down in a Sutemi, Sacrifice Throw, to hurl your opponent. After the throw, both combatants should be positioned as shown.

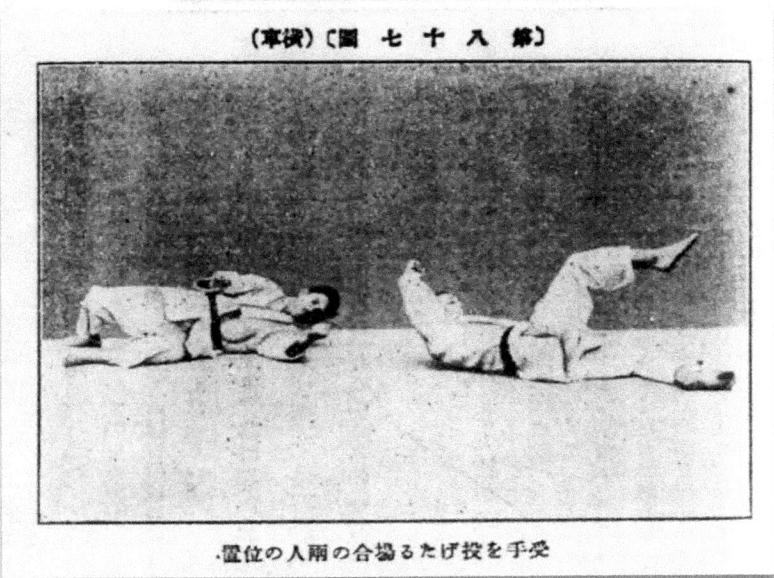

Yoko Guruma – Side Wheel Throw 1 ~ 2
Top: Step forward with your right foot, wrap up your opponent and ready to throw. Bottom: After the throw, both combatants should be positioned as shown.

Uki Waza – Floating Throw 1 ~ 2
Top: Both combatants hold each other in Yotsu, gripping under the arm and on the back.
Bottom: You then ready to do a Sutemi, Sacrifice Throw.

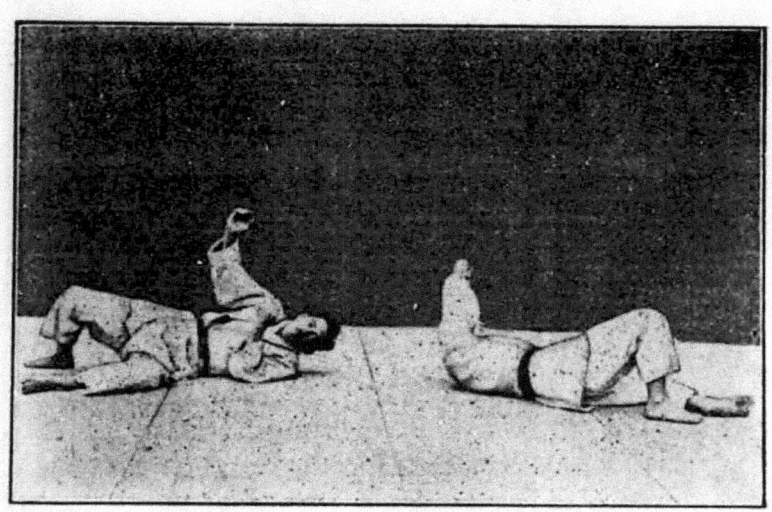

Uki Waza – Floating Throw 3 ~ 4
Top: Throw your opponent over your left shoulder, which is pressed into the ground.
Bottom: Both combatants positioning after the throw.

Maeda thoroughly enjoyed the demonstration since he was working with a second-degree black belt. This meant he could move and throw more aggressively. Further, he cut a swath through the students that had developed fundamentals, throwing them this way and that. Maeda felt like he had returned to Japan and the style of training done in his home country.

Before Maeda arrived in the UK, the Judo club at Oxford was extremely popular. They even held a Kohaku, red team versus white team tournament, in conjunction with the London Judo Academy. Several teams of ten would compete for a grand prize. The Japanese ambassador to the UK at the time, Komura, offered a silver cup as a prize.[19] In the previous Kohaku tournament, the University Club won and they still display the silver cup.

---

[19] Komura Jutarō 小村壽太郎 (1855~1911) was the ambassador to Britain from June 1906 to August 1908.

Overall, Maeda was impressed with the student's training regime. Their posture and attitude were excellent. While the building they trained in was old, the decorating was understated, so it had a cultured air about it.[20]

Maeda was planning on spending the night at Oxford University so after the demonstration he had time to see the sights. The next day he returned to London and found that the re-establishment of the Judo Academy was going nowhere fast. Maeda continued to teach the student who was interested in both Judo and Gekken.

One time, the student took Maeda to Whitehall just outside London and introduced him to an old gentleman named Steers.

---

[20] The Cambridge University Boxing, Fencing and Jujitsu Club
"Demonstrations of the Japanese art of Ju-Jitsu formed the most fascinating items in an attractive programme, among those assisting being two of the best exponents in this country, Maida (sic) and Yukio Tani, from the Japanese School of Ju-Jitsu, in London.
With the assistance of Mr. G. T. Lemon, Clare, Maida demonstrated the art of disturbing the balance, as practiced by the people in the country of the chrysanthemum, and Yukio Tani, with Mr. E. T. Busk, King's, as a medium, illustrated methods of causing surrender by discomfort, or, in other words, of getting an opponent in such position that he cannot move without giving his rival an opportunity to inflict bodily injury. Maida and Mr. Z. Horikiri, a Japanese Non-Collegiate student, gave an exhibition of Shobina Kata —the ancient art of disturbing the balance by fancy throws—and there were also exciting Ju-Jitsu encounters between Mr. Z. Horikiri and Mr. E. Morse, King's ; Yukio Tani and Mr. E. A. MacNee, Clare ; and Maida and Yukio Tani. In the contests between Englishmen and Japanese, the former, although invariably the bigger men, were no match for the Japs in dexterity. The display between the two professionals was especially exhilarating, although it was explained to the company that the men were not putting forth their best endeavours, as, if they did so, they would be likely kill one another."
-*Cambridge Independent Press*
June 14th, 1907

Steers wearing a Judo Keikogi on the porch of his house

The Gymnasium, Showing the Bath Sunk in the Floor

The Dwelling-House of an Apostle of Health 1909

An Old Gentleman Crazy About Judo[21]

Steers, the old gentleman, was well-known as a curious sort of man. He lived in a house on top of Whitehill, about an hour and a half by locomotive from London. Steers despised the cutthroat world of London and built his residence atop Whitehill so he could have empty space on all four sides of his house. He was wealthy but his house had an elegant, informal style. He also paid to have a Dojo built on his property and even slept on a Tatami mat as a bed. Apparently, he curled up on hard Tatami mat at night wrapped in just a wool blanket.

Maeda heard that on warm, clear nights the curious fellow would sleep in the grass outside. His Dojo fourteen Tatami mats in size, and this is not just a description of size, Steers actually imported Tatami mats from far off Japan.[22]

Typically when describing a Dojo in a foreign country it is carpets spread over the floor. However these are not ideal for rolling smoothly. However, Steers, who perhaps had more money than sense, had paid to ship real Tatami mats from Japan. You have to admire the man's tenacity.

As far as Steers' daily life went, he rarely ate beef or pork and his diet consisted primarily of rice, fish, vegetables and chicken. Instead of gravy he used soy sauce. If he ate Sashimi and made Japanese style beef stew then he would basically be Japanese.

Once, Maeda asked Steers how he came to enjoy Japanese things.

---

[21] William E. Steers (1857?~1930)
In 1903 Steers set sail for Japan, where he befriended E.J. Harrison and began training in jiujitsu. Returning to London the following year, Steers joined the Golden Square dojo of former Bartitsu Club instructor Sadakazu Uyenishi. There he made the acquaintance of Gunji Koizumi, who had recently arrived from Liverpool where he had been briefly affiliated with the highly dubious Kara Ashikaga School of Jiujitsu.

[22] The size of a tatami mat varies slightly by the region of Japan, but a standard tatami mat is about 1.8 X 0.9 meters, or about 5.9 X 3.0 feet. In Tokyo, they are a little smaller, about 1.76 meters by 0.88 meters. Steers' Dojo seems to be about 22.68 square meters or 244.4 square feet.

The elderly gentleman replied, "I vacationed in Japan and went to Yokohama. There I saw a Judo demonstration and became obsessed with it. While I wanted to start training right away, my schedule wouldn't permit it. So, after returning home, I got in contact with a Judo instructor in London."

At this point the eccentric gentleman had been training for close to two years. In the course of training he had dislocated his knees twice, so nowadays he wrapped his knees with bandages when training with Maeda. He was about 58 years old, but his body was in good shape and he was very energetic. He also regularly read translations of the Forty-Seven Ronin, Bushido and works by Socrates.

Steers was knowledgeable, saying, "This art of Judo that your fine country developed is more than just learning throws, holds and joint locks in order to develop the body. Judo also places importance on developing the mind. Thus, it is of great value."

To this Maeda responded, "It is as you say, this is the core idea behind Kano Jigoro Sensei's Judo. He always says you should be working to develop and improve both your mind and your body.
During training, Maeda endeavored to use his imperfect English to explain what he had learned from listening to Kano Jigoro's lectures and how Steers was using it to improve. The elderly gentleman was delighted with this and responded, "I will make an effort to be conscious of those things." Steers continued, "I would like very much to travel to Japan again and study directly under Kano Sensei. I would also like to tell him what I think about Judo."

Maeda very much liked the man as they both seemed cut from the same cloth.

The elderly gentleman added, "I believe that studying Japanese Judo should be the foundation of the education of English youth."[23] The elderly gentleman would wake up early every day and go the Dojo. Once there he would train for thirty minutes before removing all his clothes and jumping into a large tub filled with water that he had placed in his garden. After cooling himself for thirty minutes, he would lay out in the sunshine for twenty minutes. While relaxing he would eat some fruit, before changing into Japanese style clothing complete with straw sandals or Geta. Then he would walk

---

[23] In his paper Steers encourages the adoption of Kodokan Judo.

around his garden.

Next, he would go into his office and read the newspaper or one of his favorite books. Around eleven he would eat breakfast. His house was built atop a small hill so he could see clearly in every direction.

From his house you could see farms and men cutting wheat in the fields. In the distance dark specks on the horizon were all that could be seen of the next closest villages. Steers liked being well away from the dirt and grime of the city. Indeed the view was like a painting. If you used a telescope, on clear days you could see smoke rising out of London. Living in such an environment, breathing in fresh air was invigorating. Doing Judo in such an environment could not help but keep you healthy.

When travelling to Steers' house, Maeda would catch the train heading out of London and stay at Whitehill for three or four days. Steers fed him well and over the course of his stay Maeda would gain four or five Kin, 2.4~3 kilograms/ 4.3~6.6 pounds. Maeda heard that before he arrived in the UK that Mr. Nanma had also been a frequent guest at the elderly gentleman Steers' house.[24]

Steers was very dedicated to Judo and progressed a lot faster than would be expected because he was clearly thinking carefully about everything. He may have been 58 years old, but when he undressed he was well muscled and seemed to have a youthful body. He was about 1 Sun taller than Maeda so about 5.5 Shaku, 5.5 feet/ 1.7 meters tall. He was about 4 or 5 Kin heavier than Maeda.

Turning to Maeda he said, "You shouldn't live in a smoky, dusty city like London. You can live here for however many years you want." Maeda was flattered by the man's sincere offer and felt the old man was like his father. They had become good friends.

Maeda soon became busy with the re-opening of the Judo Academy but he still travelled out to the elderly gentleman's house once a week and stayed for two or three days. Maeda would also teach seminars every other week, staying for four or five days in various places. At any rate, his summer was full of activity. The

---

[24] Nanma Norihiro 南摩紀麿 (?-1936) He was said to have developed Seioi Otoshi. Which was also known as Nanma Otoshi 南摩落.

English members of the former Judo Academy were beginning to return from continental Europe or the seashore where they had gone to escape from the heat. Before they began trying to restart the Judo Academy in earnest, they took up an offer to go to such-and-such a place in the highlands and watch a traditional strength competition. From what Maeda could gather the event was quite interesting with many competitions that were unique to this area. So, five of them, Maeda, two Japanese Judoka and one of the English Judo instructors, set off by train.[25]

The Japanese Self-Defense Instructor

The Highland area was quite a distance from London, requiring a thirty-hour locomotive train ride. It was quite a journey and while not uncomfortable it was extremely dull. They arrived the day before the event started.

There were a lot of different events, some of which were very unusual.[26] First they rolled out four longs about 1 Shaku, 30 centimeters/ 11.8 inches, in diameter and about 2 Ken, 3.6 meters/ 11.9 feet long. Four men then stepped forward, each picking up one pole and raising it vertically in the air. After scampering four or five paces forward they throw the pole forward. The pole would fly through the air and land on the top end. Then, with momentum

---

[25] During a visit to Japan in 1912 Steers was awarded Shodan by the Kodokan. In December of 1918, Steers gave a lecture titled *A perfect manhood and Judo of the Kōdōkan* which he submitted to the UK department of education.

[26] "Grand Demonstration of Ju-Jitsu"

(...) from the Japanese School, Oxford Street, London – Tarro Miyake, Champion of Japan; Yukie (sic) Tani, who has never been Defeated; Professor Maeda, Government Instructor; and Hirano, the Lightest and Cleverest Wrestler in the World.

Open Challenge to Any Wrestler in Great Britain. Military Display by a Detachment of the Scottish Horse. The Usual Athletic and Other Events. The Celebrated Kirkcaldy Trades Band will be in Attendance during the Day.

-Dundee Courier 1907

carrying it forward, the end the men were holding initially would swing up so the pole was standing vertical before falling in the direction of the throw. Whoever was able to throw their pole the furthest is the winner.

Clearly executing such a throw takes a lot of practice, however first you must have the strength to pick up the long pole and hold it vertically. In other words, if you are not a large powerful man from the Highlands of Scotland this is unlikely to be an art you can hope to imitate. That day a wrestling champion from Scotland won the pole toss.

The next event was a horse-riding event. All the competitors had earthenware bowls on their heads and the riders all tried to smash their opponent's earthenware pot.

There was also a demonstration of traditional Scottish dances.

Clearly this kind of festival cannot be seen anywhere else. Finally, there were wrestling events. After the events were done, Maeda and his group did a Judo demonstration, showing both Kata and Randori, free sparring. Seeing the demonstration inspired the wrestlers to want to get in on the action. However, despite being much larger than Maeda and the other Japanese Judoka, the wresters got thrown hither and yon, rolling about with a *Bata Bata* sound of uncontrolled limbs hitting the mats. The wrestlers were also forced to tap out due to the various chokes and joint locks that Maeda and the other Judoka applied. This ended up being the best part of the day. Following that, the dining hall opened and they were treated to a fine meal before boarding the train that evening for London.

Having returned to London the group began to search for a way to restart the Judo Academy, but none of their plans seemed to get any traction. Places where the rent was cheap were in bad locations and they would have to build their own changing rooms and bath. Nicer places were too expensive to rent considering the amount of income they were expecting from lesson fees.

The main problem seemed to be gathering enough money, and even with the former students of the Judo Academy pooling all their money, it wasn't enough. Maeda, casting a wider net, asked the men who had been running the Dojo up until now, "Does anyone know anyone who might be willing to help?"

One day, while visiting the house on the hill in Caterham he asked the old gentleman for advice. "Well, I want to become your top student so you had best start your own Dojo!" And with that, the negotiations started, taking advantage of Steer's knowledge and monetary resources.

First, the elderly gentleman introduced him to a famous Englishman. The man was an instructor of something called "Japanese Self-Defense Techniques," which was based on a curious theory that went,

"The utterly mysterious Judo developed by the Japanese people makes them the most fearful people on earth. When dealing with them the only way to win is to use Judo." [27]

Basically, he was teaching Judo to the people of his country. The Dojo was a small place located between the second and third blocks of the famous Piccadilly circus. It was a small Dojo so Maeda would run classes on days the Englishman did not, which ended up being four times a week.

As it turned out the introduction went even better than expected. In exchange for rent, Maeda would assist the Englishman with teaching Judo. In the end, Maeda was able to set up his own Dojo without paying a penny.

Interestingly since the students that took lessons from Maeda were the ones who had been training for three years at the Judo Academy, two or three of them were about Shodan level. As Maeda began training in the shared Dojo, it soon became apparent that Maeda's classes were interesting and had an energetic atmosphere. It was clear the Japanese Self-Defense instructor couldn't hold a candle to the skill of Maeda's students. Perhaps realizing this, the Self-Defense instructor asked Maeda, "If we can work out a good time, would it be possible for my students to train with you?"

In short, the instructor was asking Maeda to teach his own

---

[27] "Professor Vernon-Smith", who advertised jiujitsu classes at his Anglo-Japanese Institute of Self Defense (3 Vernon Place, Bloomsbury Square). He seems to have employed Sadakazu Uyenishi as well as "a staff of expert instructors teaching gymnastics, boxing, wrestling, fencing, la savate etc."; very little else is known about it, or about Vernon-Smith.

-The Mystery of the "Japanised Englishman"
BartitsuSociety
2020

students and he himself would join in the training as well, offering no instructions to his students. The scene of a Japanese Self-Defense Instructor admitting his art is somewhat lacking and allowing his students' names to be ripped from his register and placed in another teacher's register seems like a parody of how martial arts Dojo work.

At any rate, the "Judo" taught by this instructor was a curious thing indeed. He seemed to have some basic knowledge of boxing, which he incorporated into his lessons. In short, what he taught was a mishmash of Judo and boxing. Interestingly, one of Maeda's students was an amateur boxing champion. So, whenever that student participated in lessons, the self-defense instructor would never use any boxing. Again, the situation was quite absurd.

The boxer in Maeda's class, despite being an amateur, was still good enough to win the local amateur championship, and he was also about Shodan level in Judo. Since, as a boxer, he was able to move around the ring and position himself deftly. Interestingly, he said of Judo, "Judo is several levels more advanced than the sport of boxing. No matter what angle you approach if from, Judo is clearly the better system. I can attest to this based on my own experiences. Whatever free time I have I am going to devote it to Judo."

For his part, the Japanese Self-Defense instructor went around saying, "Right now my Dojo is featuring a Japanese Judo champion by the name of Maeda Mitsuyo!" This interesting form of promotion resulted in a dramatic increase in the number of students. So it came to pass that the owner of the Japanese Self-Defense Dojo, without consultation had begun using Maeda to advertise his business.

This resulted in a large increase in students joining the Dojo. However, many of the new students felt that since they were learning an art developed in Japan, they should learn from a Japanese person. So for the most part, the students attended Maeda's classes. In fact, on days when Maeda was not there, many students would complain. "I thought a Japanese man taught these lessons!?" Before Maeda had begun teaching at this Dojo, there was a certain medical doctor that took lessons from the Japanese Self-Defense instructor. However, after a few weeks of training, the doctor didn't feel he was learning much so he switched to learning from Maeda. In fact, the doctor took to Maeda's lesson and began to take his lessons exclusively.

In fact, at one point the doctor approached Maeda and said,

"There is no need for me to continue seeing the Englishman for instruction. I would very much like to attend your classes exclusively." Then he handed Maeda six months of lesson fees in advance.

Maeda completely understood where the man was coming from, however this would be stealing another person's students. However, when Maeda brought up the subject with the Japanese Self-Defense instructor, the man replied the way you might expect an English gentleman to,

"My dear fellow, don't be absurd! Take the money. Clearly the student should pay the person who instructs them. The fact is the doctor has me at my wits end! He pesters me endlessly with questions about variations on techniques, and I find it exhausting."

This is a fine example of the relationship between the Japanese Self-Defense instructor and his "golden advertisement." Maeda was under the impression that most of the students would be the children of wealthy elites, however this turned out not to be the case. One man was a low-paid office worker at a bank who went to work with a lunchbox on his waist. There were also clerks that worked at shops who used part of their meager salaries to pay the monthly lesson fee. Quite a few would stop by on their way home from work to train for twenty or thirty minutes before continuing on home.

From noon until about three o'clock in the afternoon there was an elderly fellow who came for lessons. It was during this sort of lesson that Maeda could really see the steadfastness of the British. Any Japanese person who wanted to start Judo at forty years of age would have been laughed at. Further, the man, despite being grandfatherly was no doubt forcing his wife and children to endure stories of how, "If I were a younger man..!" while drinking his evening Sake.

The Steadfastness of the English

While there was a tendency among American students to quit Judo training after a week, this was rare in English students. Since they would continue training long enough to develop an understanding of what the art of Judo was about, they became more interested in it. This lead many of the English students to understand that Judo is the best method for developing the body and for self-defense. This is completely different to how the Americans approach Judo training.

Maeda was sure that Judo would continue to flourish in the UK. Part of the reason is the English understand that there is a difference between Judo and Western-style wrestling. In other words, they have Judogan 柔道眼, an eye for Judo, which makes it easier for them to win in duels. Since the English students had this understanding of Judo, it meant that Maeda couldn't let his guard down.

As for overall ability, there were several English practitioners who were about Kodokan Shodan level. Considering the fact that these English Judoka stood over 6 Shaku, 180 cm/ 5'9", in height and were big framed, their power was tough to match.

Amongst the students, one man was a UK wrestling champ who had frequently dueled Japanese Judoka in public bouts. He knew his way around a Dojo and was very crafty. He was skilled and a tough opponent in duels.

When Maeda was not teaching at the Dojo he would be out and about in London making grand challenges and fighting all comers. The challenge Maeda issued was, "Any challenger that can last more than ten minutes in the ring with me will get 100 yen for each minute thereafter. Further, If I am defeated I will pay a challenger 10,000 yen."

However, despite the dramatic challenge, Maeda had not had to pay out any money. That being said if some of the members of Maeda's Dojo were to challenge him, he may well have to pay a 100 yen a few times, though there was no danger of him having to pay 10,000 yen.

As it turned out, the challengers tended to be self-styled tough guys or strong men that didn't possess any real skill. In fact, most of them didn't even have the endurance to last ten minutes. Most of the tough guys that took on Maeda did so on the spur of the moment, with visions of the 10,000 yen prize in their eyes. No doubt they were thinking, "It doesn't matter how quick he is, a 5.4 Shaku Jap Judoka who only weighs 19 Kan won't be a match for a 6 Shaku 30

Kan Englishman.[28] In addition, even in the unlikely event I lose, the Japanese Judoka is the only one putting up money so I won't have to pay a penny! Winning would mean I get 10,000 yen!"

The potential windfall was too delicious to pass up. Thus, as you might expect, many men would spit on their palms and rub them together and bravely mount the ring thinking, " As long as I can last ten minutes I can collect 100 yen!"

No doubt many of the challengers were already dreaming of how they planned to spend the 10,000 yen, though these dreams would prove to be for naught. Usually, the first man up would seize Maeda's sleeve fiercely as if by taking hold of him they were snatching the 10,000 yen off the table. Maeda would of course make use of the fact that his opponent was holding on firmly and rotate him around a few times before throwing the man a terrific distance. Then Maeda would lock the man up.

This of course meant that the next challenger would be more cautious, which made him easy prey for Maeda. By now all of London knew of an extremely powerful Japanese Judoka who couldn't be beat. They became interested in some of the specific techniques Maeda was using and wanted to see if they could escape from them. What they wanted to do was test these techniques and resist submitting. The minute rule would not work in this case.

The reason was there were quite a few challengers who would enter the ring multiples times against Maeda. They tried out various defensive strategies to try and buy time until ten minutes were up, thereby collecting 100 yen. This meant Maeda was going to have to extend the time limit to fifteen or twenty minutes or else he was going to have to pay the hefty one-hundred-yen prize money. That being said, there was the danger that Judo would begin to resemble wrestling if he changed the rules. It would mean he was no longer introducing Judo and people would criticize it saying, "Judo is boring!" Further, biased newspapers would likely run articles saying, "If you can hold out for ten minutes, you can defeat Judo."

In addition, there were some people saying that by promising to

---

[28] 5.4 Shaku = 1.6 meters or 5.4 feet
6 Shaku = 180 meters or 6 foot
19 Kan = 71 kilograms or 157 pounds
30 Kan = 112 kilograms or 248 pounds

pay money, Maeda was in violation of Bushido, the way of the Samurai, however outside Japan, betting on duels was the accepted practice, so there was no bad influence.

The truth is, if Maeda didn't offer a wager he wouldn't have been able to find anyone willing to challenge him. Since Japanese Judoka don't start fights, Maeda offered a 10,000 yen prize. There were plenty of people who heard about the 10,000 yen prize and then saw the tiny Jap and thought, "This is the guy that hasn't been defeated!?" and were inspired to try and take him out. Thus Maeda had to prepare himself to face a person of unknown strength, who might be from any corner of the globe and battle that person with every ounce of his strength. He had not a penny to his name, but he was fully committed to engaging in one all or nothing duel after another.[29]

The only thing comparable in Japan would be Dojo Yaburi, when a martial artist seeks out the strongest member of another school to demonstrate their technique is superior. Or maybe how Samurai long ago hunted down and battled supernatural creatures.

Some curious things happened in course of these challenges. Here is one example: Maeda once issued a challenge, "If anyone can escape my joint lock once I've applied it will receive ten yen." At this announcement, one man leapt at the chance. The man, who was the image of the perfect English gentleman, declared, "I'll try that! Go ahead and put the lock on!" Since his challenger was a decent looking man of middle height, Maeda was somewhat reluctant since the man might be injured. Meanwhile the crowd was shouting, "Do it! Do it!" The English gentleman calmly walked toward Maeda, rolling his sleeve up and seemingly unafraid. Maeda still wasn't sure about this man, but the Englishman seemed obliging and lay down on the ground, offering his arm.

So, Maeda set up for the arm bar, but obviously did not yank on it quickly. As he was applying it, Maeda felt the English gentleman's arm twisting in his grip and so when Maeda tried to lock his arm, there was no effect. The man then stood up, meaning that Maeda was hanging ineffectively on his arm. Maeda tried to

---

[29] Jijo-Jibaku 自縄自縛 Generally speaking this means "caught in one's own trap" however in this case it seems Maeda is fully committed to following through.

reposition but to no avail, so he released.

Maeda felt like saying, "That was just a demonstration so I wasn't putting as much force as I typically would during a duel…" however Maeda realized that he had made a mistake with his lack of attention and his opponent had got the better of him. If he started making excuses now it would only appear cowardly. So, he swallowed his pride and took the high road, offering the gentleman the promised ten yen. However, the gentlemen surprised Maeda by laughing and waving the money off. Though the English gentleman didn't say anything, Maeda could tell by the expression on his face that he was admonishing Maeda for underestimating an opponent.

With a bit of a self-serving grin he said, "Actually, I have done a bit of Judo training." Then he turned to the onlookers and addressed them, "I was initially suspicious of this man's claims and wanted to confirm that he was, in fact, a real Judoka."

Maeda could only laugh and say to the onlookers in response, "Good sir, the fact is I was holding back so I did not apply the lock as I usually would. If this had been a duel and I applied that lock as we dropped down there would be no way for you to escape it. While I do admit defeat, I would very much like to try again without my previous restraint!"

The gentleman grinned and replied, "I am perfectly aware of that and let me just say that I was in no way disparaging your technique. Clearly, if you yanked on my arm, I would have been unable to escape. Applying such a technique in the middle of a duel is one of the subtleties of this art. I did not step forward in this public duel in order to claim a ten-yen prize. The public still thinks of Judo techniques as being very mysterious and often misunderstands them. So, I would very much like people of my generation to learn Judo. When I first started training Judo, I felt that there was no other system that so effectively exercised every part of the body. This is a wonderful system developed by the Japanese. However, it is unfortunate that many in the UK feel they cannot train in this art since it is from Japan."

He continued, "Since you did not yank on my arm roughly to apply your lock you allowed the people watching to understand how the technique is applied, so they ca in a real situation. And for that I am grateful. Perhaps from your perspective, allowing me to escape was a blemish on your reputation. However, I don't think that is the case. By allowing an opponent to escape once, it shows that with enough training anyone can escape. Since this isn't a real bout, it cannot be considered a defeat for you." He explained clearly to the spectators.

Maeda replied, "There may be a thousand people that can see what you are talking about, however there are also a thousand that cannot. Thus, some of the people who saw you slip out of my armlock are thinking. Is Judo really so effective? Therefore, does this not obstruct what I'm trying to teach?"

The English gentleman replied in a chivalrous way, "That is of course part of it, buy now why don't you try again. This time we can both fully commit ourselves." Maeda answered in the affirmative with a, "Yosh!"

With that the gentleman again lay down. Maeda then applied the lock for real, yanking his arm back with a *Gu!* sound of something being extended. This time the English gentleman could not escape. His face contorted in pain the man shouted *Maita!* I give! When Maeda released him, the English gentleman rose again and addressed the onlookers, encouraging them to take up Judo. Thanks to this gentleman, several good students joined the Dojo and Maeda was again forced to learn a lesson about not underestimating any opponent.

Another time, Maeda was doing a demonstration and was showing how to apply chokes. After the demonstration he offered a challenge, "If anyone can escape from my choke I will give them twenty yen!" A young man in the audience wearing a cloth cap immediately volunteered. He looked like a laborer and, quite unlike the previous English gentleman, he simply wanted money.

Maeda advised the man, "If it starts to hurt, just clap your hands." So, Maeda began the choke, however the man didn't clap. Thinking the man was stronger than he seemed, Maeda increased the pressure, however the man still didn't clap. Finally, Maeda realized the man wasn't clapping because he was unconscious.

Maeda quickly used his resuscitation technique to revive the laborer. When the man's eyes opened he said, "I just had the most wonderful dream! At first it was a little painful and right when I was thinking I couldn't take it anymore, I got a wonderful feeling all over. Wow, I got twenty yen just for that!? This is a great way to make money! I will have to come here every day!"

While he was quite an amusing fellow, Maeda had to set him straight. "You didn't escape, you collapsed and died. I had to resuscitate you to bring you back to life, so there is no way you are going to get twenty yen."

"Oh, is that what happened?" the man laughed. "I feel pretty good after my attempt to get twenty yen!"

While he was laughing heartily his hand moved to the back of his pants as if he was searching for something when he got a curious look on his face. "Looks like I sat in some water…"

Maeda glanced at him and said, "That's not what happened, let's talk in the back, before any of the other spectators notice. Go over to the restroom."

However, the man continued searching the ground trying to find the source of the water. Inevitably, the crow noticed and someone shouted, "Hey there! The back of your pants are wet! Looks like you pissed yourself!"

Everyone began roaring with laughter when they saw the outline of his wet butt on the ground. After the demonstration Maeda saw the laborer again asked, "How did it feel?"

"It turns out what felt good was me pissing myself!" Maeda roared with laughter and tossed the man a five-yen coin. Which the man caught with delight. "Have a drink on me!" Maeda said.

Joe Carroll (?~?)

Joe Carroll was born at Hindley Lancaster and laid the foundation of his reputation while quite a lad. He has probably engaged in more contests than any other wrestler. He has met and defeated Jack Smith of Manchester, Peter Gotz and Tom Connors and at the Alhambra won Lord Lonsdale's Cup, which carried with it the middle weight championship of the world.

Battle 21
The Lawless Man

That fall, Maeda had a week-long Judo seminar at the theater near Victoria Station in London. He set up a sign outside that said, "Taking all comers! Challengers welcome!" At this point, Maeda was well-known. So much so that he was head and shoulders above the other Judoka as far as name recognition. Even to those Japanese Judoka that arrived before Maeda considered him the champion. Thus the people that challenged him were some of the strongest men in the UK, making for lively bouts. They were each warriors that could slay a thousand men.[30]

They were men such as Jack Marden, Joe Carroll and Eugene. All of these men were victors of numerous knock down drag out fights with Japanese Judoka. Amongst them Joe Carroll, an English wrestling champion of middle height, was particularly skilled. He was a famous wrestler known as "the kid." Though the other wrestlers were a rank lower in status and fame, they were all burly powerful men who had taken on Judoka dozens of times, therefore there were few people unfamiliar with them.

Previously, two or three Judoka had wrestled these men but were unable to submit them after fifteen or even twenty minutes, so they each lost two hundred yen. There is even a rumor that a certain Judoka refused to duel them when they applied. However refusing a challenge is not the same thing as being defeated. In a true fight, a Judoka would use every method at his disposal to take down a larger opponent including kicks and strikes. However, in this case the difference in size was just too great. Even if the Japanese Judoka threw or attacked with joint locks, these would be ineffective on their opponent due to the size difference, so there is a valid reason to refuse such contests.

So, as it turns out, while Maeda was more than willing to take on any of these men, they seemed to think they didn't have a chance at winning. In fact, all the challengers seemed to be thinking about was the best defense strategy, one that would be appealing to a crowd.

---

[30] Ikki Tosen 一騎当千 One mounted Samurai that can take on a thousand men at the same time.

These proposals started with conditions like, "If Maeda loses, he must pay a thousand yen." Or sometimes it was "ten-thousand yen." Other proposals stipulated, "If the duel lasts the full ten minutes or full fifteen minutes, then Maeda must pay a hundred yen." There were some even more elaborate proposals like, "Every minute after the first eight minutes, Maeda must pay ten yen."

Other proposals were awarding the amateur wrestling league a gold medal. It seemed every wrestler had an elaborate proposal. From the perspective of a Judoka, if you can't defeat an opponent after ten minutes, then you won't be able to defeat him with ten times that amount of time. If the contest was going to be decided by throws, then this wouldn't be a problem. However, these contests were decided by submission using joint locks or chokes. That being said, while throws are a Judoka specialty, there is also a danger when using them against wrestlers. This is because foreign wrestlers are very adept at grabbing the legs and taking down their opponents. The reason this is a problem is that no matter how many times you say that hooking the legs and pulling your opponent down does not count as a throw, Western wrestlers refuse to admit this. Apparently, a while back, the longtime English manager of a Judoka agreed that both parties should accept each other's definitions of techniques in order to make the winner of each duel clear.

After arriving in the UK, Maeda was sure to confirm the rules were agreed to in advance in order to prevent misunderstanding. While he was in America, many events stipulated that pressing your opponent's shoulders to the ground was a win. However, that meant Maeda was unable to employ sacrifice throws. At the same time, the Western wrestlers scoffed at the notion of wearing a Keikogi, meaning it was difficult to apply Judo techniques. In the end, such contests became rather dull wrestling versus wrestling instead of wrestling versus Judo. Thus, while throwing techniques will not directly lead to a win, they were still a valid method of setting up a finishing technique.

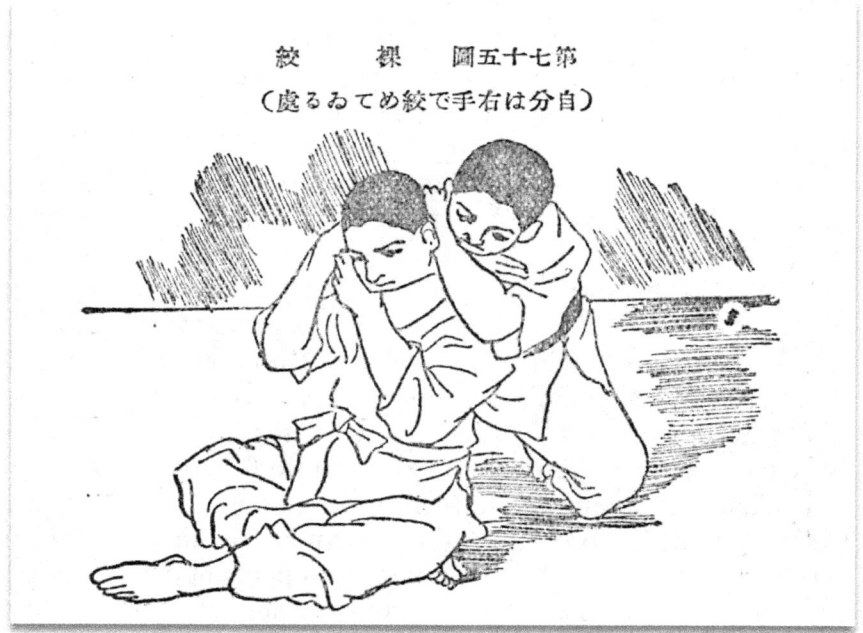

Hadaka Jime, Rear Naked Choke

While Western wrestling did not have as many technical moves, it does contain some joint locks, throws and chokes. Among them are the stranglehold, a technique that looks similar to Hadaka Jime, Rear Naked Choke. While the stranglehold is more or less banned in wrestling matches when dueling with Judoka. This choking technique is regularly employed, therefore other than Judo kicking and striking techniques, Maeda free to employ all the throws, chokes and locks in Kodokan Judo.

While the wrestling techniques used by wrestlers were inferior to Judo techniques, the men were twice Maeda's size and had wrestled with Judoka dozens of times. That being said, sometimes there were fellows who felt they didn't have a snowballs chance in hell of winning through technique, so they attacked like a Samurai possessed by a wild boar, therefore Maeda could never let his guard down.

Thus, Maeda arranged for a public exhibition with the above conditions at a theater near Victoria train station. For the first two days Maeda made short work of his challengers, but on the third day he was set to face a tough fellow. However, as Maeda walked onstage, a well just dressed gentleman sitting in the audience stood and approached the ring accompanied by a giant man. The gentleman then declared in front of everyone that he wanted a duel between Maeda and the man, who apparently was a wrestler. The crowd was watching with interest.

The challenger was a large man but no one seemed to know who he was. The crowd shouted, "Who is that guy?" "He looks very strong!" Maeda responded to the gentleman's request, "I am sorry, but I already have a challenger for tonight. Would tomorrow be acceptable?" Despite this refusal, the man pressed on, explaining that they had traveled a long distance and insisted that the duel happened here and now.

At this point, the crowd was becoming excited about the prospect of seeing this large wrestler in action. They started shouting, "This looks like a great match! Fighting! Fight!" They also began jeering, "Are you scared of losing?" It seemed as if it was impossible for Maeda to extricate himself from this situation. The call to fight by the first heckler had now been picked up by the whole crowd, which was forcing Maeda's hand.

The man Maeda was scheduled to fight tonight was one of the aforementioned three foreign wrestlers. He wasn't particularly well known, so Maeda politely explained the situation and asked to postpone their bout. Eventually, a deal was reached and Maeda faced off against the giant wrestler. Seeing this, the audience applauded their approval. The referee stood and the time keeper signaled he was ready. The match began and the two sides closed on each other. Maeda's challenger, though he was a giant man, attacked in a typical wrestling fashion, moving to take Maeda's legs.

Maeda brushed this attack aside and seized his opponent's Keikogi. The man was very strong, so Maeda had to be careful since he seemed like he could easily last the full minutes. Maeda decided he needed to take out his opponent quickly, so he attacked with Tomoe Nage.

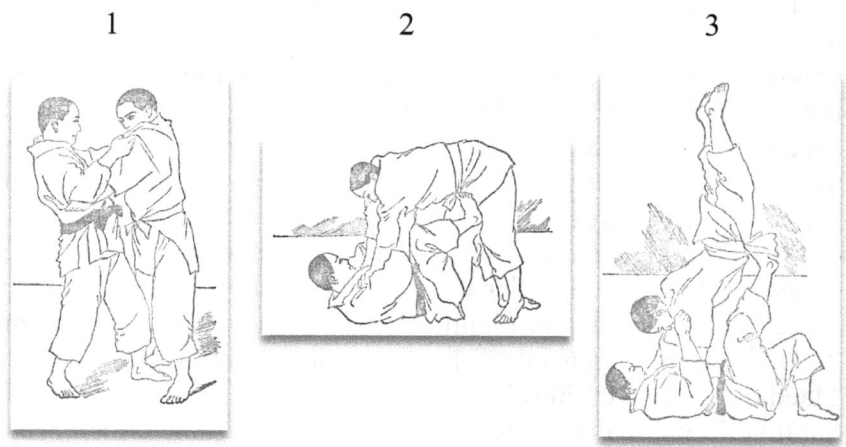

The Sutemi Waza, Sacrifice Throw Technique, Tomoe Nage
Judo: An Illustrated Instructor's Guide 1941

As the giant rose after being thrown, Maeda seized his lapels and threw with Tai Otoshi, following him to the ground and moving into an armbar. However, the giant was extremely strong and shook his arm free. Maeda, however, continued his assault, leaping behind the man and began choking with Okuri Eri Jime.

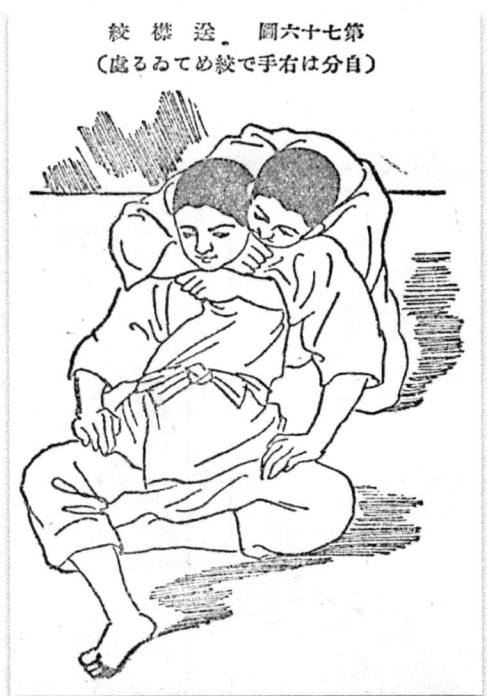

Okuri Eri Jime, Sliding Lapel Strangle
This shows how your right hand should choke.
Judo: An Illustrated Instructor's Guide 1941

Though it was a choke, there was a lot of complaining from the audience that this was unfair, so Maeda switched his attack to the giant's arm, yanking it hard into a lock. This time the giant wasn't able to escape and with that the match was over. The total time was 3 minutes and 20 seconds. The crowd, which had previously been critical of Maeda for not immediately acquiescing to the giant's challenge, were now lambasting the defeated man, shouting things like, "You are worthless. Less than worthless!" Maeda ended the event for the day after that match.

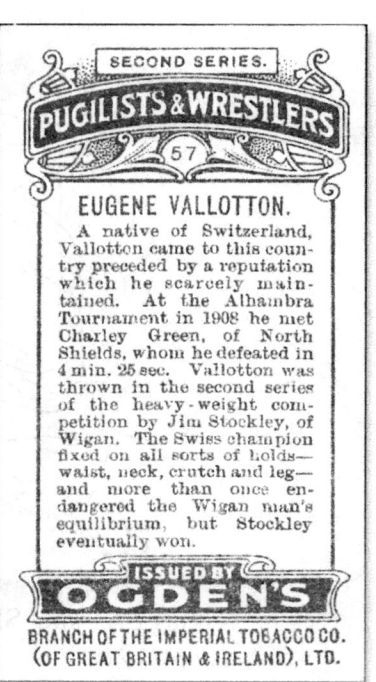

Eugene Vallotton (?~?)

A native of Switzerland, Vallotton came to this country preceded by a reputation which he scarcely maintained. At the Alhambra tournament in 1908, he met Charley Green of the North Shields, whom he defeated in 4 minutes 25 seconds. Vallotton was thrown in the second series of the heavyweight competition by Jim Stockley of Wigan. The Swiss champion fixed on all sorts of holds, waist, neck, crotch and leg, and more than once endangered the Wigan man's equilibrium but Stockley eventually won.

Battle 22
The Ozeki of the English Wrestling World

On the fourth night of his exhibition Maeda was set to battle a man named Eugene, one of the previously mentioned three wrestlers. When the referee introduced Eugene the capacity crowd went wild. However, when the match began, the audience became strangely quiet in anticipation of this duel. In fact, they were so quiet it seemed like they were all holding their breath and sitting with their hands gripped into sweaty fists. Maeda attacked first, but Eugene knocked it aside. Next, Maeda set up a perfect throw, but the man rolled deftly and got back to his feet. Maeda then attacked with more throws, looking to transition to an arm bar, but Eugene was able to slip free every time. Further, if Maeda gave Eugene an opening he would immediately exploit it.

Eugene's attacks were easy to understand and deal with once he started to apply them, however Maeda realized the contest seemed destined to extend beyond the ten-minute time limit. Eugene had wrestled Judoka dozens of times, however all of them had favored Hiari Kumi, left grip, while Maeda favored Migi Kumi, right grip. Maeda could tell his opponent was having trouble adjusting, since he was being thrown with greater frequency than when he dueled other Judoka. Of course, this weakness was not just because the different way of gripping, Maeda was clearly one rank more skilled.

At some point the match passed the five-minute mark. Then the seven-minute mark. Maeda needed to submit Eugene within the next three minutes. Eugene, for his part realized he was not going to win, so he switched to defense. Suddenly, however he dropped to the ground while pulling on Maeda's sleeve. He succeeded in yanking Maeda towards him and in that moment Eugene wrapped both legs around Maeda's neck, locking him tight. As Maeda tried to slip out Eugene reached around and grabbed for Maeda's collar in order to choke him. However, whether intentionally or by accident in the heat of battle Eugene had grabbed Maeda's hair and was yanking it. At this the audience all leapt to their feet cheering and shouting. Half the crowd was encouraging Eugene, "You beat that Jap!" While the other half yelled, "Pulling hair is illegal!"

Eugene had Maeda's head scissored between his legs and a firm grip on both his sleeves, a difficult situation to escape from.

Maeda had one hand holding the hand Eugene was gripping his hair with but his other hand was free. So, Maeda seized the hand pulling his hair with both hands and pushed while pulling his neck in. At the same time, he pushed Eugene's legs with all his strength and managed to free himself. Once free Maeda snatched one of his opponent's legs in a lock. Maeda had a firm grip so escape for Eugene was impossible, however the man didn't seem inclined to tap out, instead he endured what must have been an extremely painful lock. At this point eight minutes had elapsed and if Maeda let go of Eugene's leg it seems doubtful he would have another chance to get another lock within two minutes.

Maeda put everything he had into the leg lock. Eugene was clearly in pain as he was grinding his teeth and sweating like he was in a fire. At that point, the time keeper announced one minute remained. The words, "One-minute remaining!" pierced Maeda's heart, however they seemed to reinvigorate Eugene. Maeda felt the man would let his leg break rather than submit. Eugene suddenly twisted his body, rolling over. This was a fateful error as rolling his body caused his leg to twist further, and he could no longer endure the pain. He tapped out, signaling his defeat. The time was 9 minutes 36 seconds and the victory went to Maeda Mitsuyo.

The crowd which had been cheering Eugene now changed, and were unified in their applause for Maeda. As the cold sweat that covered Maeda's body indicated, this had been the most difficult duel he had fought thus far. While he had never been in danger of losing, his opponent was a skilled veteran with a massive advantage in strength. This prevented Maeda from stopping him in a short amount of time. If this had been a life or death battle, it would not have lasted such a painfully long time.

Defeating a larger opponent in a short amount of time without injuring him is quite difficult. After changing his clothes, Maeda returned to the stage and again great applause broke out. Everyone wanted to shake the winner's hand on the way out, and by the time Maeda made it to the street, he was exhausted and sweating. The next day, when Maeda went to the theatre, his supporters, who explained the event to the public, had three letters. It turns out that they were all from fans and basically all the letters said the same thing. One person was obviously furious and wrote, "When he pulled your hair, how come you didn't demand the match be stopped?" Another obviously angry person wrote. "A gentleman such as yourself should not allow cowardly behavior to go unpunished, but forcefully expel it!" Maeda felt this was an example of the large heartedness of the English people. If one of their countrymen wins due to underhanded means then they will scorn him. For them, it is better to fight, clean and lose. On the other hand, Americans are the complete opposite. They will back one of their own no matter what he does.

This doesn't apply to the general populace who watch from the top gallery of the theater rather it applies to the gentleman from the middle class and above. They are principled and look at more than just who wins or loses a match.

Migi Yotsu (Sumo)

Migi Gotai (Judo)

Battle 23
The Clever Veteran

On the fifth day of the exhibition, Maeda was set to duel the man who was originally scheduled for the third day. "The match isn't worth writing about, I defeated him." Maeda said.

On the sixth day, Maeda had a duel with Jack Marden. Rumor was that Jack ranked higher in skill that Eugene, who Maeda defeated on the fourth day, so this would be a big fight. Maeda noticed when they met in the changing rooms and exchanged greetings that his opponent's movements had a certain deftness and precision. Jack was energetic and seemed to be about the same height as Eugene, 5.9 Shaku. The moment the fighter appeared the crowd went wild with applause. It was quite a scene. The timekeeper shouted the start and the two combatants shook hands and engaged. As soon as the bout began, Maeda could tell by the way Jack moved that he was a nimble fighter. Jack apparently had decided that he would launch the first attack, because he leapt straight at Maeda and tried for Tomoe Nage. However, it was clear that Jack had not learned this technique properly from a teacher. Instead he was mimicking a technique he had encountered many times when dueling Judoka. Over the years he had been thrown many times by this attack and had begun to use it himself. However, his foot was not shoving with enough power and his pull was weak. However, clearly the man understood that the contest would be decided by chokes or joint locks, so he was no doubt anticipating transitioning to one of those attacks after a throw. Thus, he was well-prepared to defend himself and possibly even able to keep Maeda at bay for the full ten minutes.

That being said, Jack was a well-known figure in the wrestling world and if he simply defended the whole match, he would be the laughingstock. Even if Maeda were to lose in such a situation, the crowd would look favorably on his efforts and Jack would be embarrassed.

So, when Jack attacked with one of his half-learned throws, Maeda could use that as a chance to attack with his own throw and then transition to a lock or choke. Maeda could also tell that his opponent was used to Judoka engaging with Hidari Kumi, thus Maeda was able to execute beautiful throws starting from Migi

Kumi.

The next time Jack tried to pull off a Tomoe Nage, Maeda evaded this so deftly it made a mockery of the attack. Maeda then went for a Yoko Sutemi, which he executed well. The followed that up with a textbook, Uki Waza, then a fine-looking Yoko Gake.

Maeda then made point of moving in to grab Hidari Yotsu.[31] Since Jack excelled at responding to attacks from this grip, he too grabbed Hidari Yotsu and set up for a Yoko Sutemi, which was just what Maeda was expecting. Maeda now had complete freedom to attack with Yoko Otoshi, Tani Otoshi, Sumi Gaeshi or any other technique he chose.

After having a sure-fire throw spoiled, Jack was in a fury and he attacked with a left Tani Otoshi that was so well set up and executed that Maeda felt he was momentarily in danger. While neither combatant can be defeated by a throw, it was more than a little embarrassing for a Dan ranked student of the Kodokan to get thrown in such a manner.

While Maeda tried to keep a good balance of attacking and defending, he seemed unable to finish his opponent off. For his part Jack really didn't like Maeda's habit of engaging Migi Kumi, and would frequently call out to Maeda during the match, "Grab left!" It may seem like it is a ploy to get you to move a certain way, however if someone is resorting to calling out, "Take a left grip!" it basically means they have given up.

However, despite the fact that this is a seemingly cowardly request, foreign wrestlers have no compunctions about calling out to each other, asking their opponent to attack in a certain way.

On the fifth day of the exhibition, Maeda was set to duel the man who was originally scheduled for the third day. "The match isn't

---

[31]*Migi-yotsu* 右四つ is when your right hand is slipped under your opponent's left arm to seize his belt, with your right arm outside your opponent's right arm. *Hidari-yotsu* 左四つ is the opposite. Your left arm is inside the opponent's right arm. This hold is called Migi (right) and Hidari (Left) Gotai, or Defensive Stance, in Judo, however typically opponent's grab the back of the Keikogi instead of the belt. Since Maeda did both Sumo and Judo, he presumably could be using either method.

worth writing about, I defeated him." Maeda said.

On the sixth day, Maeda had a duel with Jack Marden. Rumor was that Jack ranked higher in skill that Eugene, who Maeda defeated on the fourth day, so this would be a big fight. Maeda noticed when they met in the changing rooms and exchanged greetings that his opponent's movements had a certain deftness and precision. Jack was energetic and seemed to be about the same height as Eugene, 5.9 Shaku. The moment the fighter appeared the crowd went wild with applause. It was quite a scene.

The timekeeper shouted the *Begin!* and the two combatants shook hands and engaged. As soon as the bout began, Maeda could tell by the way Jack moved that he was a nimble fighter. Jack apparently had decided that he would launch the first attack, because he leapt straight at Maeda and tried for Tomoe Nage. However, it was clear that Jack had not learned this technique properly from a teacher. Instead he was mimicking a technique he had encountered many times when dueling Judoka. Over the years he had been thrown many times by this attack and had begun to use it himself. However, his foot was not shoving with enough power and his pull was weak. However, clearly the man understood that the contest would be decided by chokes or joint locks, so he was no doubt anticipating transitioning to one of those attacks after a throw. Thus, he was well-prepared to defend himself and possibly even able to keep Maeda at bay for the full ten minutes.

That being said, Jack was a well-known figure in the wrestling world and if he simply defended the whole match, he would be the laughingstock. Even if Maeda were to lose in such a situation, the crowd would look favorably on his efforts and Jack would be embarrassed.

So, when Jack attacked with one of his half-learned throws, Maeda could use that as a chance to attack with his own throw and then transition to a lock or choke. Maeda could also tell that his opponent was used to Judoka engaging with Hidari Kumi, thus Maeda was able to execute beautiful throws starting from Migi Kumi.

The next time Jack tried to pull off a Tomoe Nage, Maeda evaded this so deftly it made a mockery of the attack. Maeda then went for a Yoko Sutemi, which he executed well. The followed that up with a textbook, Uki Waza, then a fine-looking Yoko Gake.

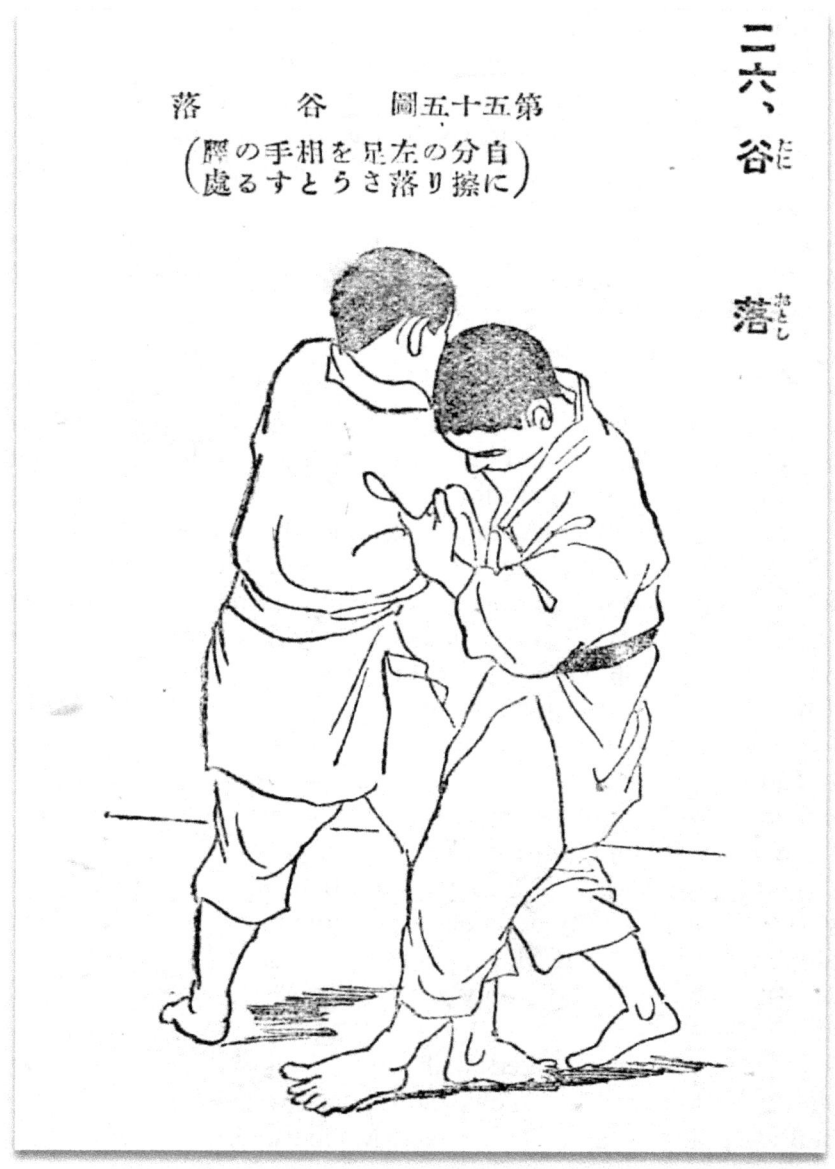

Tani Otoshi – Dropping into the Valley
"Use your left foot to make contact with your opponent's calf.
Maintain contact as you drop him down."
Illustrated Instructor's Guide to Judo 図解柔道教範
By Oda Akemichi 小田明道 1941

Maeda then made a point of moving in to grab Hidari Yotsu. Since Jack excelled at responding to attacks from this grip, he too grabbed Hidari Yotsu and set up for a Yoko Sutemi, which was just what Maeda was expecting. Maeda now had complete freedom to attack with Yoko Otoshi, Tani Otoshi, Sumi Gaeshi or any other technique he chose.

After having a sure-fire throw spoiled, Jack was in a fury and he attacked with a left Tani Otoshi that was so well set up and executed that Maeda felt he was momentarily in danger. While neither combatant can be defeated by a throw, it was more than a little embarrassing for a Dan ranked student of the Kodokan to get thrown in such a manner.

While Maeda tried to keep a good balance of attacking and defending, he seemed unable to finish his opponent off. For his part Jack really didn't like Maeda's habit of engaging Migi Kumi, and would frequently call out to Maeda during the match, "Grab left!" It may seem like it is a ploy to get you to move a certain way, however if someone is resorting to calling out, "Take a left grip!" it basically means they have given up.

However, despite the fact that this is a seemingly cowardly request, foreign wrestlers have no compunctions about calling out to each other, asking their opponent to attack in a certain way. Maeda simply nodded and said, "Yosh!"[32] and grabbed Hidari Kukmi, and showing his intent to attack with Osoto Gari. But this was just a feint and he switched to a Migi Kumi and attacked with Tsuri Kumi Koshi, throwing Jack so hard it surely rattled his teeth.

Jack got up from that throw furious and stopped asking for Hidari Kumi. However it was clear to Maeda that throws were not going to decide this match. Once when Maeda ended up underneath the man he tried for Juji Jime and other chokes, however his opponent always managed to slip free. Maeda tried to pull Jack in close but he used a wrestler's standard defense of pushing on Maeda's legs and tucking his chin in. At one point Maeda's concentration slipped and Jack almost got a leg lock.

At this point over six minutes had passed. After the five minute mark the timekeeper would start calling out the time in ten second intervals. Maeda had been under Jack for more than thirty seconds

---

[32] "Very well" "Here we go"

at this point, trying to pull him into a lock. It seemed Maeda wasn't going to be able to lock him up from below, so he slipped out and stood up. Maeda moved in and started to attack with a left grip, but the switched to a right grip and attacked with Migi Okuri Ashi Barai. Though Jack was on the verge of being thrown, he seized Maeda's sleeve and managed to stop the technique.

Maeda shifted his body around and when his opponent stepped forward to brace himself, Maeda attacked him with Hiza Guruma. Jack leaned into Maeda, pushing with both hands. The fact that Jack was able to respond to Maeda's attack in such a fashion was clear evidence his opponent had done a lot of training and was highly skilled. Maeda responded by using the force of his opponent's two-handed push by jerking Jack's left sleeve with all his might, Maeda dropped down onto his right side, throwing his opponent with a Yoko Sutemi.

The throw had so much force that it threw Jack off the stage and he and Maeda crashed into the orchestra pit. Almost immediately Jack began grappling with Maeda again. It may have been because he was angry or because he took a hard fall off the stage, but Jack was attacking in a disorganized fashion. However, the referee stopped the two and made them return to the stage. Jack released his grip and the two climbed back onto the mats. While the time keeper had stopped the clock while they were grappling in the orchestra pit, only three minutes remained.

Though Maeda was in no danger of losing, he was concerned about whether he would be able to submit his opponent within the allotted time. Taking the man down to the ground had proven difficult and he was in danger from Jack's leg locks. Maeda was going to have to continue to throw the man and then seek an opening to drop on top of him and take a joint lock. Since his opponent had dueled with Judoka frequently, he was familiar with the typical Judo attack of grabbing with Hidari Kumi and throwing before transitioning into a left arm bar. Maeda would have to feint that attack and then switch to a right technique and put Jack's right arm in an arm bar.

The first thing Maeda needed to do was get a solid Ippon throw. Maeda caught hold of Jack and threw him with Yoko Sutemi, but when he tried to follow up with a right arm bar, Jack rotated his body and rolled out. Maeda then attacked with De-Ashi Barai, and succeeded in bringing his arm down to the ground. This time Maeda tried to lock up Jack's left arm. At that moment the timekeeper, who had been calling out the time at ten second intervals announced that 9:30 had elapsed. There was no time to stand up and try and throw the man again and then try for another lock. Seeing a chance, Maeda seized Jack's right arm and put on a lock. If his opponent escaped, time would run out.

Maeda was well-versed in how to lock up an arm and his opponent would not be able to escape using only his left arm. Maeda pulled with all his strength and his opponent tapped out. At that moment the timekeeper shouted, "Ten seconds remaining!" A few seconds later a second voice shouted, "Ten minutes!" However, Maeda did not release the man until he had tapped tow or three times. No doubt the man would be complaining later, but in such a close contest Maeda could not afford to release after only one tap. He had to endure three seconds of the lock until the ten minute time limit was called.

Standing victorious, Maeda found he was covered with a cold sweat that surpassed the one after the fight with Eugene. Maeda was never in danger of losing due to skill, only having the clock run out. In the final moments of the match, everyone was cheering but when Jack tapped out and the timekeeper shouted, "Ten minutes!" everyone stood up and cheered for Maeda in an explosion of sound that was deafening. Since throughout the duel Jack had fought with kill, his name could frequently be heard shouted out and some spectators even threw 1 or 10 Yen coins up on the stage.

After changing clothes, Maeda emerged to find a sea of people waiting to shake hands with him. As he moved through the crowd, a mother holding a baby approached him and said, "Will you please kiss my baby?" This drew everyone's attention, which flustered Maeda. Despite being embarrassed, Maeda felt he couldn't refuse, so he kissed the child. Apparently the mother hoped that if a strong person kissed her child, her child would grow up to be strong. Luckily Maeda didn't have to kiss the lovely young mother, or he would've been in trouble.

Maeda's Cowardly Fellow Countryman

Maeda would have to have another day to duel, however though the exhibition was set to last for a week, the next day was Sunday, which is a holiday in the UK, so the exhibition ended on that day. Therefore the match with the most famous of the wrestlers Joe Carrol would have to be postponed for three weeks. In the interim, Maeda decided to go visit the Naval Yard at Portsmouth. He wasn't able to find a challenger there so he went to observe the Judo training at the Naval Academy.

Previously, this Naval Academy had contacted the Judo Academy on Oxford street to send someone to teach Judo three times a week for a year. Following that year, the school appointed one of the students to be the teacher and did not renew the contract with the academy. Maeda tried two or three times to arrange to train with the naval cadet who was leading training, but wasn't able to.

It turns out, just before Maeda arrived in the UK, this naval academy was in negotiations with a certain Japanese Judoka living in the UK for an instructor. The Japanese Judoka did not want to travel that far, so he asked Ono Sandan to go in his place. Ono Sandan agreed, however the Judoka had a rather strange request, "I would like you to say that you are me when you go there to teach." While the Judoka requesting this of Ono Sandan was an experienced practitioner, Ono Sandan's skill level was far superior. In the end, Ono Sandan politely refused the request.

So, why did the Naval Academy did not approach Ono Sandan directly? His skill level was far superior to that of the Judoka who had been living in London for a long time. However, as is often the case, the first Japanese Judoka to win a bout in a foreign land to becomes the "Top Judoka from Japan" irrespective of how skilled he may be. Therefore Ono Sandan, despite being both a stronger and technically superior Judoka, was almost entirely unknown, while the Judoka who had been living in London for a long time was quite famous. While in Japan people are able to differentiate the various merits and demerits of Judo Sensei, this is simply how things work in a foreign country, so they are unable to judge the skill level of a given Judoka.

Maeda and his fellow countrymen for their part respected the Judoka that had moved to London before them, seeing them as pioneers. Thus, despite the fact that Maeda was more skilled, he in no way tried to take over the school, poach students or otherwise disrupt the fields Maeda's predecessors had carefully sewn. Further, Maeda had no intention of travelling overseas and putting on another Sumo wrestler's Fundoshi and expect the Japanese that arrived previously to support him.[33] That is why he arranged for public duels with top local wrestlers in order to display his prowess and thereby increase his notoriety.

This is the Western style of doing things. Of course there are those who still advocate for the old concept of Bushido who completely misunderstand the point of holding for profit public events where the spectators pay a fee to enter and anyone can challenge the person who is holding the event. In Japan's Feudal Era we had Dojo Yaburi, where a martial artist would challenge the top student at another school, hoping to make a spectacle of defeating the best student. There was also Gozen Shiai, where all the martial arts of Japan would send their best members to duel in front of the Emperor and other high ranking officials.

On one hand if you are nothing but a promoter using dishonest means to collect money then that is to be deplored, however going on stage and engaging in a fair and balanced duel is an honorable way to conduct an event. It is extremely unfortunate that Ono Sandan lost a chance to secure a position at the Naval Academy. Maeda stayed two nights at the Naval Academy before returning to London.

---

[33] Tanin no Fundoshi de Sumo wo Toru 他人の褌で相撲を取る "To borrow another person's loincloth to Sumo Wrestle" Refers to profit at someone else's expense or To rob Peter to pay Paul or To take risks with other people's money.

The Lovely Students at the Boarding School

Maeda resumed teaching his students three times a week at the Dojo he was borrowing from the Japanese self-defense Sensei. One day, he received a request to teach Judo at a junior high school in Chatham, which was about a two hour locomotive ride from London. He agreed to teach there two times a week.

On his first visit, Maeda noted that the school was on a small hill, somewhat removed from the other houses. Maeda found the location invigorating. None of the students commuted to the boys' school, rather, they all lived in a dormitory. When he first met them, the boys seemed quite reserved and clearly the sons of middle and upper class families. Initially, Maeda was unsure if these students would be able to do Judo. However, once the lessons got started, he found they responded enthusiastically. On breaks between classes, the students would play outside on the exercise field, which was as large as a football pitch. During Judo practice, the students didn't complain at all about skinning their knees. It was the same kind of intense training that would be done at a Japanese school.

This is something that the middle and upper class British gentleman excelled at. The upper classes were completely enamored with intense, physically and physically demanding sports. The principal of the junior high school was a football fanatic, and the children at this school didn't eat fancy sweets made of Mochi, pounded rice cakes, or Yokan snacks from the Eitaro company.[34] You don't find a lot of students that isolate themselves in their rooms when classes are done.

Students attend this school starting around the age of 13 or 14 until they are around 17 or 18. They are innocent and quite inquisitive. After Judo training, the boys would sit in a circle around Maeda and pepper him with questions. While the questions weren't particularly difficult, Maeda sometimes got stuck due to his language ability. The students, realizing their teacher was having trouble, would rephrase their questions. A lot of questions were along the lines of, "How can I become stronger?" or "In Japan, do kids our age play soccer and do Sumo wrestling?" Maeda answered. "In Japan, students do a variety of sports including baseball, soccer,

---

[34] This company is still in business today.

tennis and crew. Plus, most students also take Judo and Gekken fencing lessons. These are all paid for by the Physical Education Funds." In response to the students asked, "How come this school doesn't recommend all students take Judo? It would be nice if they paid for it as well!" Maeda mentioned that some schools set up, Judo clubs for training outside of lessons. The students surprised him by establishing the club at their school on their own, using their own pocket money that they would normally spend on snacks and light amusements to run the club. Maeda was mightily impressed.

One of the roughest and most energetic of the students was a boy who was planning on becoming an Admiral in the Navy. The other boys all called him, "Togo! Togo!" Maeda found it amusing that they called him Togo instead of Nelson. Eventually the 40th year of Meiji 1907 drew to a close and the winter vacation began. Since the junior high school was going on break, Maeda decided to head to Birmingham for a week long seminar and exhibition lecture. It was an industrial town with a technical school. The town was big into sports so Maeda was surprised when he got no answer to the challenge he placed in the local newspaper. Apparently everyone was busy preparing for Christmas. However, he was approached by a man looking for a Judo instructor at a Military Academy starting in a month. The man needed an instructor for four or five students, two of whom were women. However, since the job wouldn't start until the end of January and there were only four or five students, Maeda decided it wasn't really worth his time and turned the offer down.

Battle 24
Breaking the Nose of a British Tengu

It turns out there was an Englishman in this town who had opened up a Judo Dojo. He even used a Japanese name, calling himself "Matsuda Sensei." Apparently, after training Judo for two months in London, he returned to Birmingham quite full of himself. So much so that he even put up a signboard saying he was an invincible Judo instructor. This is the kind of self-centered trickery a Tengu, or Japanese mountain goblin, would use. The man certainly held his nose high. When Maeda stepped into the Dojo, the man looked like he had been poleaxed. "Would you like to train with me" Maeda asked in a casual manner. Matsuda Sensei at first struggled to answer, but then recovered and said, "That is exactly what I would like." So the pair changed into Keikogi and faced off in the training area. The red haired, blue eyed "Matsuda Sensei" attempted to apply his interpretations of the various techniques he had learned over his exaggerated two month training session at the London Judo Dojo. However, what he was doing looked nothing at all like Judo. Maeda toyed with him for a bit before throwing him with Uchi Mata, using a bit more force than was strictly necessary. Matsuda Sensei hit his head as he landed hard.

Taking a break, Maeda joked, "You are pretty skilled!" To which Matsuda Sensei replied, "In London I trained with three or four Judoka and you throw differently from them. I can't figure out where to put in power." He wouldn't admit that he wanted to get an Ippon throw on Maeda. The man was still full of pride. In response to the brazen fool, Maeda simply scoffed, "I think the problem is you weren't trying hard enough." He added, "The Judoka in London aren't doing anything different. They were just taking it easy on you. For some reason, you took that to mean you were better than you actually were. You were strutting around like a Tengu, a mountain goblin. They figured if you got thrown violently, it would probably kill you. Speaking of which, did you hit your head? You hit your head pretty hard, eh?"

Despite this unrestrained scolding by Maeda, the man continued with his excuses. "Someone's head hit the ground, but it was not me, it was you!" In the face of this outright lie, Maeda began to despise the man. "I see. Well, then, I apologize for my mistake. If you would allow me to apply another technique, you can show me how you can defeat it." Matsuda Sensei took the bait and agreed to another duel. So the next duel started and Maeda set up Hiza Guruma. When the man lost his balance and began wobbling forward, Maeda wrapped him up firmly and threw him full force with Ura Nage. Matsuda Sensei's head and hips slammed into the ground. After being thrown. He lay on the ground, groaning for a while as he tried to focus his eyes. "How was that?" Maeda asked. Despite his defeat, Matsuda Sense was still making excuses. "The problem is the Judoka and London all use a left grip and you are using a right grip. This is extremely hard to deal with" Maeda was exhausted with the man, "That is just proof that your skills are undeveloped. It is Essential that you train both the left and right sides equally. To not do so would be idiotic. If she just continued to train in a haphazard manner, you will never become strong." Matsuda sense, for his part, didn't seem to take anything in. Maeda recalled that this utterly stupid sensei had also trained in boxing, so he proposed, "Would you like to do a Taryujiai, a cross-schools bout, your boxing versus my Judo?" But Matsuda Sensei wasn't interested and replied, "I am not interested in such a contest. On the other hand, I would like to do some real training close. And with that, Maeda left later that afternoon. Maeda returned to London.

EMPIRE PALACE
CROYDON.

Manager — EUSTACE JAY

TWICE NIGHTLY Doors open at 6.20. Commence at 6.35
8.50. " " 9.0
SATURDAYS FIRST HOUSE at 6.15 COMMENCE at 6.20

FRIDAY NIGHT, 1ST HOUSE
DECEMBER 20th, 1907.

BILLY ROSS
Middle-Weight Champion Boxer of England.

WILL MEET

YAMATO MAIDA

ROSS TO BOX!
MAIDA TO WRESTLE!

Private Boxes 12 6 & 10 6 Four Persons 7 6 Three Persons EXTRA SEATS 2/6 & 2/-	FAUTEUILS AND STALLS	GRAND CIRCLE AND STALLS	CIRCLE	PIT	GALLERY
	1/6	1/-	9d.	6d.	3d.

SATURDAYS (Second House only), Bank Holidays and Special Occasions, Fauteuils 2/-; Grand Circle and Stalls 1 6; Circle 1/-; Pit 9d; Gallery 4d. Fauteuils, Grand Circle & Stalls, and Circle can be Booked in advance 3d. extra. No Money Returned. No Seats Guaranteed. The Right of Refusing Admission is Reserved. Box Office 11 till 2 30 and during the Performance, and at PILES, High Street, Sutton

Battle 25
A Rough Fight With a Boxer

    Two or three days later, Maeda received an offer from the owner of a theater to participate in a week long tournament in a town called Croyden, which is a short distance outside London. This was on December 24th, in the final days of the 40th year of Meiji 1907. While it wasn't snowing, it was extremely cold. Maeda arrived in Croydon to find that the event was a local wrestling tournament. Every night, five or six wrestlers would fight. The plan was for Maeda to do a demonstration after the matches were over. After that Maeda would take on anyone that decided to challenge him on the spot. Then, on the final day of the contest, Maeda would take on whoever was the champion of the wrestling tournament.

    The wrestlers were men like John Carter[35] and Smith.[36] There were twenty-five wrestlers that were white, black and red and each of them was determined to take the championship prize. Maeda travelled back and forth to Croydon everyday by train, which took about an hour and a half each way. Usually by the time he got home, it was 1:00 AM. For the first three days, Maeda didn't write about any challengers for the first three days. However, on the evening of the 4th day he writes about a duel with a boxer by the name of Jack Brendon.

    Since Brendon was a boxer, Maeda agreed to box him. This would mean this would be Maeda's first boxing match. They tied on regular training gloves, but Maeda kept wearing his Keikogi for the fight. Word of this unusual dual had spread and the theater was filled to capacity. The boxer, for his part, was a local man with many victories under his belt. The crowd certainly seemed ready to see blood spilled.

    The referee shouted, "Fight!" and the two combatants closed on each other. What Maeda could take no chances with this opponent? Maeda had never been in a boxing match before, so he couldn't try and fight like he did with wrestlers, by attacking them and then submitting them with a joint lock or choke. Maeda first had to get

---

[35] This is probably referring to Jacob Carter who was a professional boxer who was active between 1907 and 1910.
[36] Kid Smith of Manchester.

close to his opponent without getting hit. Initially, Maeda tried to shoot in and grab the boxer's legs by sliding at him like they do in baseball. However, the boxer leapt back out of the way, which left Maeda down on all fours holding nothing but air. With nothing to show for his troubles, Maeda rose. The boxer took this chance to charge in and launch a full power swing at Maeda's face. Maeda instinctively moved his head to the side.

If that below had struck Maeda in the face, it probably would have knocked him out. Since he dodged, the blow only glanced off his shoulder. The crowd gulped and felt the palms of their tightly gripped fists become sweaty. The boxer didn't stop, but next drove his fist into Maeda's solar plexus with lightning speed. The blow was so fast that it didn't register in Maeda's untrained eyes. Fortunately, Maeda had kept his left hand in front of his solar plexus. That, combined with the fact that his opponent was wearing gloves, meant that the blow didn't hurt at all. Maeda realized belatedly that he had been in a perfect position to throw with Koshi Nage, but since the boxer had attacked right as he was standing up, Maeda didn't have his legs set yet and missed the chance. He was close enough to attack though, and he swept the boxers leg.

The boxer fell on his butt before scrambling back, rolling and standing up. It was difficult for Maeda to decide how to position himself. It would be very hard to close the distance. He would have to wait for the boxer to attack, block, then stick with him as he dropped back, preventing the boxer from gaining any distance. If Maeda was slow to advance and gave the boxer a chance to take even a half step forward, then he was in danger of catching an uppercut to the jaw. The boxer advanced, attacking relentlessly. Maeda moved his body this way and that, dodging the blows. When the boxer dropped back, Maeda charged in. He was able to wrap his arms around the boxer's waist and set up for a perfect Uki Koshi Nage.

Maeda was planning to mount the bucks for after throwing him, but it turned out he had executed his throw two perfectly as the boxer was tossed across the ring where he rolled and got back onto his feet. As Maeda was throwing his opponent, the boxer punched Maeda in the back. While it wasn't much of a punch, it was a testament to the man's skill and precision. Since his first plan hadn't worked, Maeda immediately switched to his second plan.

However, the boxer didn't give him any chance to get his feet set, but advanced with his left hand guarding his face and his right hand covering his solar plexus. Then he dropped his hips and charged forward in a vicious attack. The boxer aimed short punches at Maeda's face with his left hand, then swung at Maeda's side with his right. While the strikes to Maeda's head were spectacularly fast and well-aimed. Maeda was able to block them with his forearm, so they only nicked the side of his head. Maeda could certainly feel the impact of these blows, but there wasn't any pain.

Boxers typically strike with both hands. This man's left hand struck at targets of opportunity, but it was unlikely to cause Maeda any harm. On the other hand, Maeda couldn't ignore the boxers right fist. From the beginning, Maeda had been standing with his right foot forward, but he decided to switch his stance before charging in. Previously when Maeda had charged in with reckless abandon with his right foot forward, the boxer was just getting to his feet and poorly positioned but managed to charge forward with his right foot and to strike Maeda in the side with his right fist. That was something Maeda wanted to avoid.

This time, Maeda and used his right leg to sweep the boxers left leg. This took all the power out of the boxers right punch. Maeda rapidly wrapped the boxer's right arm up with his left arm then grabbed him around the waist with his right arm, so it looked like he was in a Sumo-style Migi Yotsu, and shoved him down while holding onto his right arm. Maeda then put his right arm in a joint lock, causing the boxer to submit.

Time for this match was 13 minutes and 26 seconds. This is what Maeda had to say about this bout, "I definitely won this contest, though I would hesitate to say that this win means I can beat boxers in the future. I need to win against several more boxers before I can say something dismissive, like *I can handle a boxer*. While this man was a boxing champion, there are champions at every level. Without dueling with more boxers, I am not going to develop an understanding of the nature of boxing." This was the final match on the 4th day.

Battle 26
The Grand Champion of UK Wrestling

The wrestler Maeda was scheduled to duel on the 5th day was delayed so that match was put off for another day. Therefore a duel with the young Joe Carroll was arranged.[37] Even out here in the sticks, everyone had heard of Joe Carroll, so it was no surprise that there was a big. Poster with his name on it, hanging in front of the theater. The time for the match arrived and the two fighters walked into the ring in front of a capacity crowd to loud cheers. The timekeeper was the same man as the previous bouts. He shouted, "It's time! Shake hands!" Both sides stood, walked towards the center, shook hands before separating again. Then the fight began.

Maeda's opponent was a veteran wrestler who had been champion for several years. Thus he dropped calmly into his fighting stance. The way, Carroll dropped his hips, suggested a defensive posture. However, there didn't seem to be any tension in his muscles, so it actually seemed as if he was in Shizentai, the natural stance found in Judo. Since leaving Japan Maeda hadn't. Since the since leaving Japan, Maeda had never faced an opponent with such a relaxed demeanor. Carroll had also previously fought Judoka dozens of times. A certain Judoka even confided in Maeda that Carroll had given him a rough time in their duel, so Maeda needed to be on his guard.

Maeda started by trying to grab Carroll 's sleeve and then set up for a throw. But Carroll shook this off while dropping down onto one knee. Maeda yanked his sleeve forward, but his opponent didn't resist instead. Found an opening and used the force of Maeda's pull to scoop up. Maeda's leg. Maeda tried for Tomoe Nage, but his opponent had a firm hold on his leg, so Carroll ended up with his stomach on top of Maeda. Clearly he was a wrestler who had developed strategies against Judo techniques. Carroll wouldn't release Maeda's leg once he got hold of it. Carroll's strategy meant that Maeda was caught in a variation of vertical four quarters hold.

---

[37] Maeda describes him as a Sanjaku no Doji 三尺の童子 a youth not three shaku tall. Three Shaku is about 90 centimeters or three feet.

While the vertical four quarters hold is not painful and won't lead to a victory, time is a factor in Japan. If a Judoka keeps an opponent in this position for a certain amount of time, it counts as Ippon.

Since this was also a timed event, Maeda didn't want to be in this position for any longer than he had to. Maeda needed to free his leg and extract himself. However, if he tried to rush and was careless, he would just end up wasting time. So Maeda attacked Carroll's neck, trying to apply a choke Carroll, realizing he was. Realizing he needed to defend against this, released his hold on Maeda's leg. The moment he let go, Maeda used his legs to attack. This snapped Carroll's attention back to his legs, and Maeda used that distraction to escape and stand up. Carroll stood as well, using the relaxed stance of a veteran meeting. It would be impossible for Maeda to close and attack with an Ashi Barai or Koshi Waza.

His only option seemed to be to begin with a Yoko Sutemi, and then, when Carroll stood up, throw him again with a different technique and then transition to a lock or choke. So Maeda saw an opening and threw Carroll with a Yoko Sutemi. Carroll ruled expertly as he fell, not even allowing his back to touch the ground before standing. Then, moving like a cat, Carroll feinted as if he was going to go for a neck throw before darting in and scooping up Maeda's leg. Since Maeda was aware from his previous attempt that Tomoe Nage wouldn't work, Maeda turned around and dove in the opposite direction, yanking his leg free before rolling to his feet.

Carroll charged in again, looking to scoop. Maeda's leg again. This time Maeda shoved both Carroll 's shoulders down and. Leapt backwards the next time Maeda's enemy leaned forward, Maeda seized both his sleeves and attacked with a Migi Hiza Guruma. When Carroll was thrown off balance by this attack, Maeda hoisted him up high and through with Tsuri Komi Koshi, before transitioning into an arm bar. Carroll was unable to resist this and was flipped over onto his stomach. Maeda had kept a firm hold of his opponent's sleeves, and, as he wrapped his thighs around Carroll's arm, he yanked hard as he stretched his body out in a textbook example of an armbar.

Carroll was unable to. Take the pain and struck them out with his hand, signaling defeat.

The arrangement was to pay ¥10 for every minute over ten minutes. The match had lasted for 14 minutes and a few seconds, so

Maeda owed his opponent 40 yen. If Joe. Carroll had lasted 15 minutes. Maeda would have had to pay ¥200. If Maeda's opponent had been able to slip his arm free. Maeda would have been in trouble, as it turned out, since every seat in the theatre had been filled. The owner of the theatre had collected a lot of admission fees, so he paid the 40 yen to Joe Carroll himself. The fans were cheering their approval at the match. They had seen Maeda clearly defeat a famous wrestling champion in a great matchup, so the applause was for both combatants. In Maeda's eyes, Carroll was a true champion wrestler. While only mid-sized for a foreigner, he was still a head taller than Maeda, though he wasn't one of those monsters that was over 6 Shaku, 180 centimeters /5 feet 9 inches tall.

All in all, it had been an exciting duel. Maeda thought Carroll attacked and defended in the proper way. He wasn't overly violent and didn't try to inflict pain. Instead, he looked for gaps in Maeda's defenses and utilized them. No one expected the match to last for fourteen minutes.

After the match, Carroll, Maeda, the owner of the venue, some fans and a few of Maeda's British friends gathered in the changing room to drink whiskey. According to Maeda, Karl told him the most difficult match he ever fought lasted for three days. "The match started at two pm and lasted until five pm for three straight days. Three hours a day, so nine hours in total. There were a lot of bits of coal and dust on the floor, so that made it even harder. My opponent was 20 Kin, 12 Kilograms/ 26 pounds, heavier than me and after three days, it was still a draw. If he and I had been the same weight, I would have won." With that, Corral gulped down a shot of whiskey and gave a chuckle.

Carroll told Maeda he was forty years old. Carroll also gave his opinion on Judo, "While I think Judo is unmatched as a fighting style, Judo is Judo. In our country wrestling is wrestling, which is special in its own right. I think you should come and train in our style of wrestling. It's called Catch-as-catch-can. I think there are elements that can be incorporated into Judo." He spoke in a free and easy manner and there was none of the blustering and boasting so common amongst other wrestlers who lost.

Maeda found his interest peaked and replied, "If we can find time, please teach me some things!" However, the man replied gallantly. "It won't be one person learning and the other teaching. We will both be training."

Maeda caught the 11:00 o'clock train home to London that night.

Battle 27
Plucking the Laurel Wreath From the Strong Man

The following day was the 6th day of the event and Maeda was scheduled to fight the wrestler who had been crowned champion of the tournament. Though he was a wrestler from out in the sticks, he was the champion. He was a huge man, much larger than Joe Carroll and possessed. A fearful strengths. However, when the belts started and Maeda actually engaged the man, he found the Giant was clearly, Chikara Makase, relying entirely on strength, without any technique.

Clearly, the local giant had watched several of Maeda's bouts over the past few days, and he tried to defend against Maeda's throws the same way Carroll did the previous night by dropping down onto one knee. Then, when Maeda yanked on his sleeves, he tried to scoop up Maeda's leg. Maeda responded by darting to the left, moving behind the local giant to wrap him up. The giant, despite being a champion, was surprisingly poor at imitating the moves he had seen and was pretty unskilled overall. It looked like he was pantomiming a Judo technique.

The giant was now well and truly flustered and started flailing about trying to escape. Maeda continued his attack, trying to bring him down. The giant put all his strength in a. Lunge away from Maeda, so Maeda quickly released. The giant toppled forward and started to get to his feet in an ungainly fashion. Really realized if he let the wrestler recover, he was going to use the same teak technique as before. Namely, dropped down on one knee and crawl up his leg. This wouldn't be too Maeda's advantage. So he charged after the local giant and threw him with a Koshi Waza and allowed himself to fall on top of the giant. Maeda realized not even 2 minutes had elapsed since the start of the match. If he submitted the local giant now, it would be rather humiliating. Maeda thought, "It will be shameful if the man who had just battled his way through a tournament and was crowned champion with a laurel wreath only to turn around and get thoroughly beaten in a cross-discipline match..." Further, Maeda realized the man was resigned to losing and just wanted the match to continue for a time. With that unspoken understanding, Maeda released the lucky head on the giant's arm and stood up. Since the belt was set to last for ten minutes, Maeda slowly got himself ready before attacking with two or three sacrifice throws and hip throws.

Each time Maeda did this, he would transition into an arm bar but allow the giant to escape. Finally, Maeda threw him and again took a right arm bar before quickly switching to a left arm bar and using the rebound from his. Shift to a play with full strength, the local giant immediately tapped up. The total time of the match was 6 minutes and ten seconds. His opponent, perhaps cognizant of the fact he hadn't put up much of a fight, simply shook hands with Maeda and left. Maeda had often found that defeated foes would make a lot of excuses. They would say cowardly things like, "I drank too much last night!" or "My joints are all sore from my bout last night!"

However, the giant Maeda had just faced simply gave Maeda a firm handshake and departed. The crowd of spectators also approved, and they cheered as the local wrestler walked off stage.

A Tournament With Wrestlers From Every Country

That ended the week long exhibition match. It was. Six days long, since Sunday was a holiday, Maeda returned to London on the last day of Meiji 40 1907, and spent New Year's at his hotel. He watched the celebrations and all the hustle and bustle of the city from his window. By the middle of the month, Maeda was back at the Dojo as usual, teaching Judo. One morning, the newspaper had an interesting advertisement that gave detailed information about an upcoming tournament.

"A certain marquis and a certain earl have, in conjunction with other royals, agreed to sponsor an international wrestling championship, The prize for the "large soldiers" heavyweights will be a large silver cup filled with one thousand yen in gold coins. Second prize will be four hundred yen in gold."

"First prize in the middle weight division will be a mid-sized silver cup filled with four hundred yen in gold coins. There will be no second prize in this division. For the lightest weight division, the prize will be a small silver cup filled with two hundred and fifty yen worth of gold coins for first place and no prize for second place."

In other words, the contest was divided by weight into three classes, large, medium and small. The week long tournament was schedule to be held at the Alhambra theater. The matches would begin at 2:00 PM and last until 5:00 PM every day.[38] Any wrestler who is defeated is out of the tournament. One of Maeda's English acquaintances, who was very knowledgeable, thought Maeda should enter. Had it been a Judo tournament, Maeda would have entered without a second thought, however, since the rules were for Western style wrestling, Maeda was of the opinion he didn't have much of a chance of winning. He felt confident he could take down two or three wrestlers, but his chances of winning the prize were remote. Further, if he requested that since he was doing Judo, the match should be decided by submission, however, that would be. However, that would make it seem as if there was a special rule that applied only to Maeda, and would be a bone of contention if he was crowned with the laurel wreath.

While Maeda very much wanted to unilaterally win a duel with a 1000 yen or 10,000 yen prize, the contest he was presented with would not give him that chance. In the end, he didn't apply to be in the contest. Instead, he would have to satisfy himself with observing from the sidelines, a thought he did not relish. The tournament turned out to be a huge event, with wrestlers not just from the UK, but also France, Germany, Italy, Greece, Sweden and Norway. It was very popular and many people attended.

---

[38] Alhambra Theater, London
Wrestling championship tournament. Open to the World
Catch as catch can style under the direction of Mr. AF. Bettinson, National Sporting Club
Patrons. The Honorable Earl of Lonsdale
300 pounds in Prizes and valuable cups to winners
Commencing Monday afternoon, January 27th at 3o'clock and following afternoons during the week.
Heavyweight (any weight)
Middle weight (12 stone and under)
Light weight (10 stone and under)

-The Sporting Life
Friday January 24th, 1908

Stanislaus Zbyszko

Ivan Poddubny

Joe Rogers
"The American Apollo"

William Bankier
"Apollo, the Scottish Hercules."

Dueling the Yokozuna of the Wrestling World

At the same time the tournament at the Alhambra Theatre was taking place, a certain other theatre had several large placards out in front advertising a World Wrestling Championship. It had the names of all the men participating, including the Polish wrestler Stanislaus Zbysko,[39] who weighed more than 36 Kan, 135 kilograms/ 298 pounds.

There was also a Russian named Ivan Poddubny[40] who weighed 32 Kan 120 kilograms/ 264 pounds as well as an American named Joe Rogers who was also known as Apollo.[41] He was a giant man weighing 35 to 36 Kan. The match was going to be Greco Roman style wrestling, which is a style that doesn't have any leg takedowns. Every day the newspaper had an advertisement issuing an open challenge featuring the wrestlers glaring at each other. The advertisement seemed to be saying, "Each of us thinks we are the world champion, but who in the who is the true world champion?"

While watching the matches, Maeda felt that of the three well known wrestlers, Poddubny was the most skilled. He was also the best known. Next was probably Zbysko from Poland. He was heavier than putting and certainly strong. But he wasn't as skilled as the Russian. Finally, there was Joe Rogers, who weighed about as much as Zbysko, but was 6.3 Shaku tall. However, he was by far the worst wrestler.

There was a rumor going around that he was a charlatan from New York, or maybe a police officer who was using his big size to make some money. Despite the fact that Maeda had never heard of him, he was referred to as "New York Champion." The wrestlers had all put up 12,000 yen in guarantee money with the promise that the winner would take all. However, it turned out the American had dueled with a no-name Swedish wrestler at a different theater and earlier in the week and, despite the fact that the Swedish wrestler weighed only 26 or 27 Kan, 98~101 kg/ 214~223 lbs, he was able

---

[39] Stanislaus Zbyszko (1879 ~ 1967)
[40] Ivan Poddubny (1871 ~ 1949)
[41] Joe Rogers boxed and wrestled. He was trained and managed by Hall of Fame boxing coach Tom O'Rourke.

to last fifteen minutes in the ring with the American and thus collected a hundred yen prize.

The American was scorned in the newspapers and it became clear to everyone he was a charlatan. This meant the whole winner-take-all agreement began to fall apart as the American tried to get the newspaper company to return the 12,000 yen entrusted them. The other two wrestlers flatly refused and the back and forth recriminations played out in the pages of the newspaper every day. Frankly, the newspaper stories surrounding this event were extremely interesting. The stories themselves were completely uninterested in getting to the facts, instead, the paper focused on presenting the most dramatic accounts of the events. Maeda and the other Japanese quite enjoyed reading the daily updates to these stories, though they had to frequently refer to their dictionaries. The three wrestlers each had a professional manager, a person with a long history in the business. The American Joe Rogers had the famous O'Rourke as his manager, who was quite a shady character, which meant Rogers was twice as bad.

O'Rourke was currently running the Public Exercise Club in New York City. Maeda, on the other hand, was being assisted by Apollo, an Englishman who had lived in London for a long time and managed several Japanese Judoka. Since Apollo had worked with the Americans before he introduced Maeda to both O'Rourke and his champion Rogers.

Maeda ended up training Western-style Judo with Rogers twice. Truthfully, the reason Maeda was training with Rogers is an acquaintance had encouraged him to enter the Alhambra competition. Thus, despite the fact Maeda had refused twice he was now considering entering, so he thought it might be prudent to train in Western-style wrestling. Unlike in Judo, Western wrestlers didn't match up against opponents of different weights or strength levels. They focus on escaping so that their opponent can't grab hold of them. During training, Maeda was able to use the inertia of Rogers attacks to throw him. Rogers, on the other hand, was unable to throw Maeda even once. In wrestling you win by, "Pressing both of your opponent's shoulders to the ground." Maeda found that if he was wrestling a person of vastly different weight, he would get pinned in less than ten minutes. While Western wrestling requires skill, by far the most important thing is size and strength. Wrestlers do not compete against larger foes. At one point during training, Maeda was able to dart in, quickly rotate his hips around and throw Rogers with a Seoi Nage. Seeing this, Rogers manager approached Maeda. With an offer to do a match that was half wrestling, half Judo. Maeda quickly agreed to the half wrestling, half Judo plan.

While Maeda was training with Rogers, he had been pinned in less than ten minutes several times. However, Maeda felt that during a real duel, he could escape and probably hold the man off for around ten minutes or close to it. On the other hand, he felt sure he could defeat Rogers in well under ten minutes if they were doing Judo. As it turned out, the rules of engagement were for the person who won in the shortest amount of time.

With Maeda's agreement, the manager booked a certain theater in the downtown area and wagered $500. Hearing this, Maeda said he didn't have $500, however, the Englishman Apollo who had been managing Japanese Judoka for a long time.[42] Apollo stepped in and deposited the $500 guarantee with the newspaper company. Apollo was confident in my Maeda's abilities and was sure he would win. Clapping Maeda on the shoulder, she said. "I don't care if it's $1000 or $5000. If you are going to place a bet, come to me!"

After the day of the duel had been set, Rogers approached Maeda and said, "Would you mind showing me a little bit of Judo?" However, Apollo flat out rejected the request. "If you train with him it will endanger the $500 bet I've made. The answer is no." Maeda tried to change his mind. "I don't think we have anything to worry about. I will pretend to be weak." He assured his manager. But Apollo wouldn't budge. "If they see how how intense Judo training is the Americans will cancel the bet !"

So Maeda didn't train Judo with Rogers. However, at some point the American side began to complain about how the admission fees would be divided and in the end the whole event had to be cancelled. What was actually made public was that the event was "postponed until further notice," citing the duel between the aforementioned three world champions was decided. As for the battle between the

---

[42] William Bankier (1870 ~ 1949) originally a strongman who went by, "Apollo, the Scottish Hercules." He later managed several Japanese Judo and Jujutsu wrestlers, including Yukio Tani with whom he founded the "British Society of Jiu-Jitsu."

three world champions, all three had been releasing provocative statements to the press making grand claims. However, Rogers had been exposed as a complete charlatan. The other two criticized him mercilessly and Rogers had no choice but to withdraw from the contest.

Eventually the duel between the Russian Poddubny and the Pole Zbysko took place. The referee was a two time world champion in the Catch-as-catch-can style Hackenschmidt. He was a mighty man known as the Russian Lion. The duel was Greco Roman style wrestling, which didn't allow leg techniques. The Pole Zbysko came away with the victory. However, a lot of people grumbled that this distinction, this decision, stuck, apparently in the middle of the duel. The Russian Poddubny used his legs in an illegal way and was disguised. So in the end. It was the Polish man's name that was held up as the winner, however, as far as skill win. The Russian Poddubny was clearly better and Zbysko was kind of amateurish.

Poddubny the second most famous Greco-Roman wrestler in Europe after the Frenchman Paul Ponce.

Drums Announce the Beginning of the Alhambra Tournament

So with the World W Wrestling Championship over now, the Fr mentioned Alhambra International Wrestling Tournament was set to begin. The event was scheduled to run for a week starting January 28th. There were a great many European and Americans in attendance, all who had paid a great deal of money to travel to this tournament. However, while this was a big tournament, men who already held the title of champion like Poddubny and Hackenschmidt Would not be participating. Apparently this was because there wasn't a lot of prize money and they didn't think it was worth their time. There was the additional concern about what would happen if they got injured during a bout it would all have been for nothing.

There was also the issue of. How the competition was being run. The wrestlers were all split up into groups of 10. Each match wasn't best of three, rather if you were defeated once, you were out of the tournament. Thus a lot of things seemed left up to chance.

At last, the curtain rose on the first day of the tournament. The first bouts were between the lightweights, the so-called "small soldiers." Anyone who lost was removed from the competition for the following day. After that were a few middle-weight matches. One of the wrestlers was a British ex-soldier who Maeda was familiar with.

Battle 28
Destroying the Enemy With an Ura Nage

Initially, Maeda had been hesitant to enter this competition. However, his acquaintances were convinced. His acquaintances convinced him he couldn't pass up this chance and he felt his arms start to call out for action. Maeda reasoned, "If Japanese Judoka refused to strip off their Keikogi and engage in cross-discipline matches, foreigners will begin to think that Judo isn't useful. They will think a Judoka stripped of his Keikogi is like a. Kappa, water sprite, dragged out of the and up onto dry land. To prevent such bad mouthing, I will enter this tournament even though it is not my martial art. Even if I don't win, I will be able to show the audience what I can do. They will be able to see first-hand how Judo can stand against another style of fighting. Therefore, even if I am defeated, it won't be to the detriment of Judo."

Having made his decision. Maeda entered the tournament and even got Ono Sandan to agree to enter as well, as it turned out, since Maeda was 155 Kin, 93 Kilograms/ 205 pounds. He was in the middle weight division. Since Ono Sandan was 220 Kin, 132 kilograms/ 291 pounds, he was in the heavyweight division.[43]

However, on the day they were both scheduled to duel, it turned out Ono wasn't in London. Maeda sent him a telegram, however Ono replied that he wouldn't be able to compete due to unforeseen circumstances. Maeda considered the situation, "Well, I'm not going to want win either way, so I will take Ono's place as well." Thus, Maeda was set to duel in both the middle and heavyweight divisions.

For the middle weight bout, Maeda ended up being paired with

---

[43] Kin 斤 is another traditional unit of weight. 1 Kin is 600 grams or 1.3 pounds.
Kan 貫 is a traditional unit of weight, 3.7 kilograms or 8.3 pounds.

the former British sailor. Up to this point, Maeda had trained in Western style wrestling four times. However, he had lost every match in comical fashions since he would attack with a Judo sacrifice throw, meaning he defeated himself. Therefore he didn't feel he had any avenue to victory. But well, frankly, he wanted to see how far he could proceed in this cross discipline contest. Thus he wasn't discouraged, just determined to make a good showing.

The former sailor, Maeda was set to duel, was well muscled and looked very strong. However, since Maeda wasn't concerned about winning, he was ready to put everything in this fight the moment the bell rang. Since Maeda was a Judoka, he didn't use the same stance as wrestlers. The sailor was in a Western-style wrestling stance while Maeda was in a Judo stance. Like all Western-style wrestlers, Maeda's opponent was wary of Judo throws and how Judo practitioners tended to follow up a throw by circling behind and wrapping up their opponent. However, Maeda, was like a blind snake in uncharted territory so he remained in a natural stance, but ready for anything.

As soon as Maeda felt the sailor pushing, he would use that power to throw with Seoi Nage, Koshi Nage or even occasionally with Yoko Sutemi. Being thrown like this caused no end of embarrassment for the sailor. The reason practitioners of Western style Catch-as-catch-can wrestling didn't like being grabbed from behind is because if an opponent is able to hold you from behind for thirty minutes, they are considered to have dominated the match and therefore declared the winner.

In the face of Maeda's unusual strategy, the ex-sailor found he was having trouble employing any of his own techniques, and his movements showed how flustered he was becoming. Seeing an opening, Maeda's thought. "Now!" and through the sailor.

The moment he rose, Maeda slipped behind the sailor and wrapped his arms around his waist. If Maeda could hold him there for 30 minutes, he would win. However, the scene probably looked a bit strange. Maeda felt like a dog owner struggling with the leash, since he was on top and his opponent was on all fours. There were many different ways he could attack from this position, but since Maeda didn't know any of these Western wresting techniques, he simply held on.

図241 裏 投 (1)　　図242 裏 投 (2)
図243 裏投の(2)を前面から見たところ　　図244 裏 投 (3)

Ura Nage 1 ~ 4
From Ten Lessons About Judo 柔道十講
By Otaki Taddao 大滝忠夫 1959

Though he had a grip on his opponent's waist, he didn't feel it was very effective. "This isn't ideal but if I let the sailor go, he is going to turn around and try and lock me up the same way." So Maeda hoisted the sailor up and threw with Ura Nage. The throw was perfectly timed and it knocked the man unconscious.

The crowd exploded and everyone stood up, some shouting in alarm, some in scorn. Maeda was looking at the referee to see what he was going to do when Apollo ran up. He was serving as a manager of the event and said, "Please administer resuscitation and revive him!" So Maeda revived the man and Apollo raised the curtain which had been lowered to conceal the shocking scene. Apollo then explained how Maeda had administered resuscitation. "There is nothing to worry about. Any Judoka can revive a person without relying on a doctor." The former sailor, now recovered, addressed the crowd saying, "As you can see, I am completely unharmed." With that the members of the audience who had been heaping scorn on Maeda for his needlessly violent attack now completely reversed themselves and began to applauding Maeda. Thus Maeda achieved complete victory in his first match.

Truth be told, after throwing the former sailor, Maeda had immediately begun forcing the man's shoulders down on to the ground and was going for a pin when he suddenly realized his opponent was unconscious. For this wrestling event, reporters from fourteen or fifteen major newspaper companies were in the crowd, including ones from the prominent *Times of London*. All of them reported how Maeda was unique among the athletes, having won his match despite being smaller than other competitors. The papers all reported favorably on how Maeda revived his opponent. This was no doubt due to the fact that Apollo handled the explanation of Japanese Jujitsu resuscitation techniques to the reporters. So there had been no danger of misinterpretation.

As was previously mentioned, Apollo had been managing Japanese Judoka for a long time and also trained Judo since he presented himself as a manager of Judo athletes and also placed wages on matches. Apollo had not only developed an understanding of the principles of Judo, but also how to explain them to people. Another way to look at it was that it was due to Apollo's efforts that Judo was flourishing in the UK.

Today, Maeda competed in the middle-weight division, but he did not compete in the heavyweight. There were a few heavyweight matches after Maeda. However, the event closed for the day when the last one finished at around 6:00 PM.

Battle 29
The Thirty Kan Black Man, Chambers Zipps

The second day of the tournament was scheduled to begin with the lightweights and then proceed to the middle weights and finally the heavier weights. The late and middle weight matches were very interesting. The wrestlers, the wrestlers all moved deftly, throwing their opponents or getting through. It looked like a bunch of cats fighting that evening. Maeda was set to fight his first heavyweight opponent. When he saw the man, he was shocked at his size. He was a black man from the French colony of Algeria and he easily weighed 30 Kan, 112 kgs/ 248 pounds.

Chambers Zipps, americký

Chambers Zipps (1881~?)

Maeda was dismayed at the size of the man, who was named Chambers Zipps, but he wasn't here to befriend the man but to compete with him in a test of wrestling skill. While Maeda didn't see any chance of victory, he hoped he didn't lose in an embarrassing way. Maeda doubted he possessed the strength to pin the man's shoulders to the mats, but, well, he supposed he might find an opening and maybe get in a good throw.

The duel began and Zipps advanced on Maeda, but Maeda slipped away and began moving around the ring, keeping his distance. This irritated his opponent, who began to charge him recklessly. Since Zipps poor attacks left him wide open, Maeda moved in and threw it with a perfect Seoi Nage. Unfortunately, his opponent got right back up. Maeda felt he was safest when they were both on their feet, since his opponent couldn't throw him and he could look for a chance to throw his opponent. After some close range jockeying for hand position, the two combatants locked in Yotsu Kumi. Maeda feinted as if he were attacking with O-Goshi before sweeping with O-Uchi Gari. Zipps fought with all his strength to keep his balance, but eventually dropped down onto his butt. Maeda then rotated around behind Zipps to wrap him up, but his opponent went down on all fours, so Maeda was in the same situation as the last bout with his arms wrapped around his opponents waist in an awkward grip while his opponent crawled around like a dog.

Two versions of Seoi Nage
Arima's Judo Instructor's Guide 有馬柔道教範
Arima Tsumitomo 有馬純臣 1914

    Last night he had abandoned the unfamiliar hold, but he had learned a bit about wrestling, so he tried out a hammer lock. In Judo this is similar to a Gyaku Te, joint lock. So he kept his hold around his opponent's waist with one arm and applied a hammer lock with the other. At this point, ten minutes had passed, so if Maeda was able to last another twenty he would win.
    Considering Maeda was using a technique he had only half learned, holding his opponent for another ten minutes went surprisingly well. He managed to suppress Zipps until, with eight minutes left, Zipps tapped heretofore unknown reserves of power. Zipps put strength in his neck, and with a great shout stood up.
    Shortly thereafter, the referee called *30 minutes!* and awarded Maeda the victory based on his superior positioning throughout the match. Zipps wasn't happy and complaining loudly, even refusing

to shake Maeda's hand, just smirking at Maeda before leaving. The crowd didn't like this and shouted their disapproval. The next day, the newspapers only posted a list of winners and losers for the other matches but Maeda's match had a detailed article.

"An unparalleled display of martial spirit, a true Judoka from an imperial land in the Far East, a Japanese man demonstrated unquestionable skill in his victory. His was the last match of the second day and the doors closed at 6:40 PM."[44]

Fight 30
Felling a Rotten Tree

It was the third day of the international wrestling. Tournament. Following the lightweight matches, the little weight matches began. Maeda was in the fourth match of the middle weight division. His opponent was a Scottish man named Bryon, who was a champion in

---

[44] "Several Japanese wrestlers are taking part this week among about ninety others, in a championships' tournament under the patronage of the National Sporting Club at the Alhambra. Two of them distinguished themselves on 27th inst., Yamato showing great strength and easily winning in the middle weights ; and Hirano, although giving away quite two stone in weight, cleverly beating Earle in the light weights.

Next day Yamato stepped into the vacancy in the heavy weights, created by the absence of his fellow-countryman, Ono. Yamato had to meet a giant in the coloured man, Zipps, and though giving away a lot of weight, showed extreme cleverness. He quickly threw Zipps, who stayed on the mat for over twenty minutes and effectually prevented Yamato from turning him over.

After a short rest while both men were rubbed down, there was some quick work, the Japanese being extremely fast, and once slipping a hold in wonderful fashion. The bout went for thirty minutes without a fall, and the judges unanimously gave the verdict to Yamato, who thoroughly deserved it, the black man doing very little attacking. There was a full house, and they cheered the little Japanese to the echo."

-*The Singapore Free Press and Mercantile Advertiser*
24 February 1908

his village. Since this was the middle weight bout, Maeda weighed about the same as his opponent, making the match an easy one.

As soon as the bout began, Maeda began throwing his opponent with ease. As it turned out, Bryon didn't have much experience fighting Judo practitioners. So getting thrown left him somewhat dazed. Bryon had first attacked by grabbing Maeda around the waist and Maeda had responded with a left Yoko Otoshi. Continuing his assault Maeda forced the man's shoulders to the mat and got a pin. The match time was seven minutes and Maeda had achieved victory without any fuss.

The next bout was between Joe Carroll, the man Maeda had previously dueled, and another man named Stitcher. The two scrambled about for a while until Carroll finally saw an opening and scooped up Stitcher's legs and took the man to the ground. Joe then submitted him with a technique called the Half Nelson. The match had lasted 15 minutes and 15 seconds. The bout didn't end up being as interesting as Maeda would have hoped.

The fourth match was also between two smaller wrestlers. One of the men, Jack Carroll was the nephew of Joe Carroll the man Maeda had wrestled the other night. Jack was surprisingly good. Further, the man he was dueling was also pretty skilled, which made for an interesting duel. By the end the spectators' tightly gripped hands were sweating. Jack had some close calls, but in the 25th minute he completely changed his tactics and being began attacking ferociously and, with less than one minute to go until 30 minutes was up, Jack attacked with first a Half Nelson and then with a technique called a Clutch, and with that Jack Carroll was the winner.

Halfway through the middle weight belts, there was a match between a young man from Austria named Henry. He was hard as iron and had a brutal technique. He was facing off against a Swedish wrestler by the name of Charlie. Henry was not a tactician, instead relying on brute force, what we would call an Ara-musha in Japan. A warrior that charges straight at his opponents in a wild fury. Charlie, on the other hand, was guarded and careful. He was the amateur champion wrestler of London and very adept at applying techniques, what we would call a Waza-shi, master of technique, in Japan. Though he stayed on the defensive Charlie ended up being pinned by Henry in the 25th minute.

Battle 31
The Final Desperate Tactic of the Argentine Abdullah

Next was the heavyweight division, and it was Maeda's turn to duel. What Maeda wanted to do was show that a Judoka stripped of his Gi was not like a Kappa water sprite that had been dragged up on land and therefore deprived of his power. The fact that such a suspicion prevailed irritated Maeda to no end, so he was determined to show what a "naked" Judoka could do. So Maeda got ready for his match and was surprised when he discovered his opponent was another black man, this time from Argentina named Abdullah. He asked his manager why he was paired with a black man again and his manager said, "It was all decided by choosing lots." Maeda thought this seemed like more than coincidence, but he shrugged. He didn't really care whether his opponent was black or white, but he soon noticed his opponent smelled terrible, like a fox that had farted.

Maeda even commented to his friends, "I think I might get defeated by his smell!" Which made everyone laugh and someone commented, "Try to endure it!" To which Maeda retorted, "I will do my best but if I lose, but if I lost, I only lost because of the smell! The man stinks like a cage of foxes." And soon the match began.

Abdullah was slightly smaller than Zipps, but he was a lot more technically skilled. In a cheeky move, Abdullah leapt in and attacked Maeda with Seoi Nage. The audience clapped loudly in warning to Maeda, but this kind of attack was Maeda's specialty and he would be able to resist the man's throw. In fact, he repositioned and threw with and Ura Nage, over the back throw. Since his opponent was a Greco-Roman wrestler, Abdullah didn't make use of his legs. In addition to not paying attention to his own legs, Abdullah didn't try to scoop up Maeda's legs. In the end, Maeda was able to throw with a perfect over the back throw. If Abdullah had studied catch wrestling, then he might have been able to stop the throw by slipping his hand under Maeda's thigh. But he didn't.

However, once he was down on all fours, Abdullah could use any of the techniques he had learned in his long years of training his school of wrestling. In other words, Maeda's opponent was in familiar territory. Abdullah slip behind Maeda and got him in a lock called a Quarter Nelson and was dangerously close to pinning

Maeda. However, Maeda was able to twist his body around and then roll out.

Soto Muso (left) and Seoi Otoshi (right)

The moment he got to his feet, Abdullah seized him with Migi Yotsu, reaching his right arm under Maeda's left arm, grabbing his belt. The moment Abdullah grabbed him, Maeda dropped down onto his right knee and threw with Soto Muso. In Judo terms Soto Muso is similar to Seoi Otoshi. Maeda had executed the technique flawlessly and Abdullah went flying over Maeda's head before his huge body crashed into the mat, causing the floor to reverberate.

Abdullah got up, clearly flustered. Wasting no time, Maeda darted in behind him and wrapped him up. In response Abdullah dropped down on all fours again. Maeda again tried to employ the half-learned hammerlock, which is a kind of joint lock. Maeda was also familiar with the Half Nelson. But as he had tried to apply it, he realized that since Japanese have short arms, even after reaching under his opponent's armpit, his hand wouldn't reach up far enough to grab Abdullah's neck. So he temporarily gave up on the Half Nelson, since he couldn't apply it effectively. Instead, he relied on the Hammerlock. The Hammerlock is a kind of joint lock that can be very effective if applied properly. However, if Maeda relied solely on the hammerlock, his opponent would be able to concentrate solely on defense against that, a strategy unlikely to lead to victory.

So Maeda decided to attack with a Half Nelson, despite the fact that he couldn't apply it effectively, and use that attack to draw his opponent's attention. Then he would suddenly switch to a hammerlock. Having made the switch, Maeda ended up holding Abdullah's right wrist with his right arm with his left arm around Abdullah's neck in Oni Kubi Tori, taking the devil's neck. However, according to the rules, Maeda couldn't wrench the man's arm suddenly. That being said, slowly applying pressure would mean his opponent could escape.

Deciding to ignore the regulation, Maeda forced the man's arm up his back with a powerful shove. Abdullah didn't complain and the referee didn't say anything. So, while pulling on the man's neck with his left arm and pushing Abdullah's arm up his back with his right, Maeda forced Abdullah down onto the mat. If the referee said something at this point Maeda would have to back off and release and he wouldn't have gotten the pin. However, the referee didn't say anything, probably since Maeda had been in control throughout the bout, so in the end Maeda pinned the man and was declared the winner. So a win was a win and the time was twenty-seven minutes.

After the match, Abdullah complained bitterly, "He was yanking hard. He was totally out of control. It really hurts!" In the end, he refused to shake hands with Maeda and just smirked. The crowd jeered Abdullah as he walked off.

Until now, Maeda had managed to tie up victory after victory, however, the weaker competitors had all been weeded out, and all that remained were they truly strong. Further, they had all been paying attention to how Maeda was winning, considering how they would handle him if they were in the ring with him. In short, they were researching him. Up until now, Maeda had been an unknown factor and he had been able to surprise his opponents. Causing them to suffer at his hands.

However, from now on things wouldn't go as he liked.[45]

---

[45] "Slow progress was made with the great wrestling tournament at the Alhambra in London. The four outstanding contests in the third round of the light-weights competition occupied over two hours, and so it was found impossible to proceed with the middle-weights as had been originally intended. To give the spectators a good wind-up to the afternoon's sport, however, Maida Yamato, the Japanese, and Abdullah, the copper-coloured man from Argentine, were put on to settle their differences in the heavy-weights, and a good stirring bout they gave."

"Although the heavier by over 2 stone, and considerably the taller, Abdullah was soon flung on his shoulder to the mat by his clever opponent, but his prodigious strength enabled him to keep the Japanese from turning him on to his back. Yamato did not hurry himself, but bringing all his knowledge and skill to work, he gradually worked him over, in spite of Abdullah's frantic efforts to break the hold. The result was received with vociferous applause by the spectators, who were glad to see Yamato obtain some recompense for his defeat by Irelinger in the middle-weights on the previous day. Yamato's fellow-countryman, Hirano, a plucky little fellow, weighting only 7 stone 4 lb., met with defeat at the hands of P. C. Olsen, a light-haired, happy-faced Scandinavian from Newcastle. Olsen was over 2 stone the heavier and considerably the stronger man, but the little Japanese's surprising agility kept him at bay for nearly 25 minute. Hirano gave his opponent no rest, running about all over the mat, and in the most dexterous fashion slipping all the holds Olsen put upon him. He was frequently thrown, but managed to wriggle out of all difficulties, and he won the sympathies of the spectators by the smiling manner in which he took all the buffetings. At last, Olsen caught the little butterfly in a vice-like grip, and in spite of all his twistings and turnings, threw him in such a manner that he was not able to escape, while his shoulders were relentlessly pressed down upon the mat. Both wrestlers were heartily cheered at the finish, and the cheering was redoubled when the M.C. announced that the victor had requested him to announce that the Japanese weighed only 7 st. 2 lb. to his 9 st. 6 lb."

-*The Register (Adelaide, SA)*
Tuesday 17 March 1908

Henry Irslinger (1888~1954)

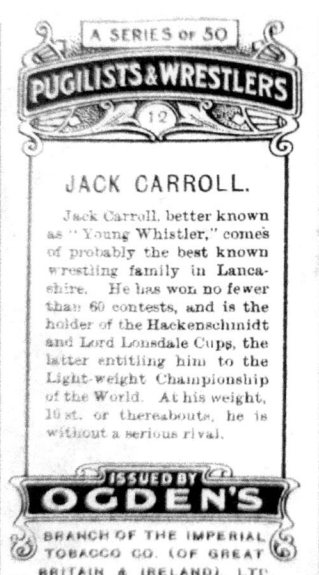

Jack Carroll (?~?)

Peter Gotz (1877~ 1959)

Battle 32
Winning by Losing

On the fifth day of the tournament, for the middle weight division, Maeda was paired with the Austrian Henry Irslinger, who was an Ara-musha, a Samurai warrior that charges straight at the enemy. He was not a technician, rather a Inoshishi-Musha, a warrior who attacked like a charging wild boar. Henry not only weighed more than Maeda, but the muscles from his chest up to his neck were spectacularly large. He was also younger than Maeda, and brimming with energy, thus a crowd favorite. As for Maeda, as he was small, had different colored hair, and practiced an unusual style of wrestling which was unlike anything the spectators had seen before. This meant that Maeda also had a certain popularity. Thus, the audience was keen to see what would happen when these two fought. Interestingly, the number of spectators had increased since Maeda's last bout and the audience was boisterous with both cheering and jeering.

The time keeper shouted It was time to begin, and the two combatants shook hands before separating and then glaring at each other. Maeda was thinking, "My opponent is a wild boar Samurai, so it would be a bad idea to wait for him to attack. As is typical in Judo. If I did that, I would likely get pinned right away. What I need to do is blunt his attack before it even gets going. So I'm going to do the opposite of what a judoka would likely do and close the distance" having made his decision, he shouted *Ya!* as he charged forward. Maeda slammed into the man and reached under Henry's left armpit with his right arm and grabbed Henry's belt. When his opponent put power in his body to prevent himself from being pushed, Maeda dropped onto his right knee and threw with Soto Muso, which is like the judo throw Seoi Otoshi. Maeda's timing had been perfect and the man went flying. However, when wrestlers get thrown, they don't resist, instead allowing their body to continue the motion before deftly rolling and standing. From the spectators' point of view, it was a beautifully executed throw, however Henry's response meant that Maeda did not end up on top, therefore lost a chance to transition to a lock.

Henry had quickly rolled over and was already back on his feet. He and Maeda locked up again, and this time Maeda wrapped both arms around the man's waist and tried to hoist and throw with Koshi Nage. Henry, however, used both hands to push on Maeda's jaw preventing the throw. Next, Maeda went for Ashi Barai, foot sweep, as he yanked both arms free. If his opponent had been a little dull it would have resulted in him falling flat on his back, however Henry used deft movements to prevent this and he managed to land on his side. While Maeda wanted to translate to a wrestling pin he feared Henry would get the better of him on the ground in a Western wrestling.

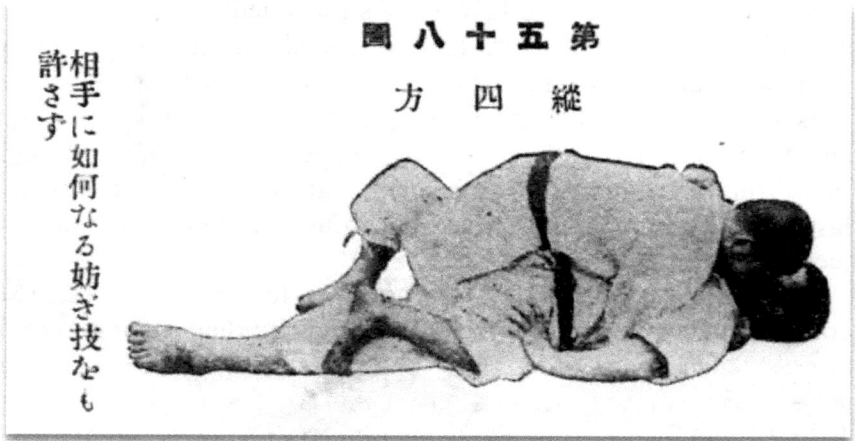

This allows you to suppress any technique your opponent may attempt.
Tate Shiho Gatame – Vertical four-quarter hold
An Easy Illustrated Guide to Judo by Arima Sumitomo 1905

So it had been close, but Maeda didn't push a bad position and backed off. Henry leapt up and, with surprising speed, advanced and slipped his right arm under Maeda's left armpit, grabbing his belt in a Migi Yotsu. Maeda immediately wrapped up that arm and dropped his opponent with a Yoko Otoshi. This was also executed perfectly and Maeda knew it. "Now's your chance!" his heart told him and he quickly transitioned into Tate Shiho Gatame. He probably would have been able to submit most wrestlers with this technique however Henry had an extremely strong neck. He flexed his body like a bow being strung. His body now resembled the curve of Drum Bridge in the Turtle Well Shrine in Tokyo.

However, if Maeda retreated from this hold he was unlikely to get another chance, so he decided to keep that position for the time being. Maeda thought maybe his opponent would tire. Just then, Maeda's opponent began using both hands to push up from below, which started to create a gap between their bodies which had heretofore been pressed together. Once that gap was opened, Henry would be able to twist out and escape. Maeda had to switch around and wrap up his neck to prevent this. So, being cautious, Maeda began to pull hard on the man's neck while pressing down with his body. Unfortunately, as this was happening, half of Henry's body and part of his head were now outside the tatami mats onto the wood flooring. From below Maeda, Henry shouted, "Outside the mats!"

Whenever two competitors end up outside the mats, the rule is that the match pauses and the pair moves to the center of the mats and take the same position before restarting the match. However, in this case, the referee remains silent. The referee, much like the crowd, was mesmerized by the spectacle. In this crucial moment where one lapse of concentration can change the course of events, the referee ignored the fact that the pair had gone off the mats. Maeda now saw his chance at victory, if he could just pin the man here.

However, from Henry's point of view, going off the mats and then having to reset in the center would give him a welcome respite. So he continued to shout, "Outside the mats! Outside the mats!" Maeda didn't care about going outside the mats, but he was sure it must hurt for Henry to have his head pushed into the hard floor. This thought may have caused Maeda, who is in the midst of attacking, to hesitate, or it may have been the sight of the referee opening his mouth to speak when, in that ambiguous moment, disaster struck Maeda.

Henry, with a ferocious burst of strength, wrenched himself free of Maeda's hold thereby escaping the jaws of death. All that work had been for nothing, and Maeda doubted he would get a second chance. As soon as Henry got up, he shot forward and seized Maeda from behind, slamming into him as if he were trying to take his revenge. Henry then began applying a Full Nelson, a forbidden technique.[46] The referee cautioned him about this, but as soon as he was out of line of sight he began putting it on again, so the referee warned him a second time. If he was warned a third time, he would lose the bout.

After that, Henry kept a sharp eye on the referee and continue to try and apply the Full Nelson when not directly in the referees line of sight. The reason he kept going for that hold was because Judoka are known to not have necks as strong as wrestlers, so Henry kept attacking that weak point. His plan was to use that technique to cause pain and wear Maeda out before using another technique to flip Maeda over and ping him. Maeda, with his weak neck, couldn't just quietly suffer until he expired. How was he to escape from this difficult spot?

At this point, Henry had abandoned the Full Nelson and was now applying Half Nelson. Henry's hand had slipped under Maeda's right armpit and extended up to grip the back of Maeda's neck. Maeda responded by wrapping that arm up, securely tucking, and rolling over completely flipping over his opponent. However, Maeda had made a fatal error since this was not his art, and he ended up flat on his back with his opponent on top of him. Maeda had rolled in a way that perfectly set up Henry's follow-up technique, and it was all over for Maeda.

It wasn't so much that Maeda got pinned as it was he rolled over onto his back. The next day, all the newspapers commented how a man new to Western wrestling had advanced so far in the tournament. The articles reported how at one point Maeda had his opponent in a tough spot and he only lost because he made an error. So Maeda got honored in defeat, almost like they were posthumous honors. At any rate, his fame had certainly increased one level.

So Maeda was finished in the middle weight division, and he wouldn't be taking home any prize money in a silver cup. However,

---

[46] Holds Barred: The "full nelson," the "hang," and all other "strangle" holds are barred. Neither will a wrestler be allowed to pull an opponent's ears, nose or toes. Nor will striking, butting, chopping, scratching or gouging be allowed, nor any other unfair act of brutality.

-Sporting Chronicle
1900's

he hadn't yet been eliminated from the heavyweight division though Maeda thought that chances of him defeating the big soldiers, as they were called, and advancing enough to take even the second prize were rather remote. Maeda was a bit glum. He had figured he had an outside chance of getting a prize in the middle weight division, since the weight differences were not as big, but he had no hope in the heavyweight division. All hope have been washed away. However, he committed himself to demonstrating what he could do on the sixth day. [47]

The wrestlers that remained on the fifth day were Maeda and three others. Earlier, Derisu the Swedish champion had taken on the Scottish champion Jimmy Esson and lost. That left just three fighters for the sixth day, Maeda, Esson and one other. Maeda realized two of the combatants would get the first and second prizes, and the third person would get nothing. His dreams of winning a silver cup were over.

So, on the sixth day, the matches started with the lightweight division. The last two lightweights who had made it through the first five days of the tournament began their duel. One of the men was Jack Carroll "Young Whistler," nephew of Joe Carroll. The other was a man named Ruden. They mounted the stage to great applause. At one point during the match when they were on the ground, Ruden slipped in between Carroll's legs and wrapped both arms around his waist. For a dangerous moment, it looked like Jack was going to get his shoulders pressed to the ground. However, Jack used his head and hands to defend against this. After another fifteen minutes, Jack got a hold of Ruden's leg with his left hand and twisted his body

---

[47] "The fourth day of the tournament at the Alhambra produced some excellent sport. There was one very surprising result, Yamato, the Japanese wrestler, who had shown such tremendous strength, being beaten by Irslinger, of Austria. Yamato did not appear in the best of health, but he found in Irslinger a man almost as strong as himself, and certainly more skillful in the catch-as-catch-can style. For the first few minutes or so Yamato was very aggressive, and several times looked like gaining a fall, but he palpably tired, and the skill of Austrian told in the end. Irslinger is only 20 years of ages."
-*The Singapore Free Press and Mercantile Advertiser*
24 February 1908

thereby escaping a dangerous situation. Then he went on the attack.

From the beginning of the match, Jack's uncle, Joe Carroll, had been alternately sitting than standing, and throughout was shouting advice, "Pull his hand there!" or "Take his leg, take his leg!" The referee and officials tried to quiet him, but he completely ignored the official and continued shouting advice. Seeing a relative of one of the combatants frantically encouraging their fighter no doubt caused those around to begin to sweat with sympathetic worry. So barely ten minutes after starting after switching strategies, Jack Carroll was able to pin Ruden and get the prize money for the lightweight division.

The middle weight final Joe Carroll versus Peter Gotz

The middle weight final was between Joe Carroll and the German Peter Gotz, who had been living in London for a long time. After Joe Carroll, he was the most well-known wrestler, though he was younger than Joe. Most people, including Joe Carroll, thought Gotz was a different fighter than he used to be and that this would be a tough match. Gotz had trained Judo extensively and had merged what he had learned with wrestling to create his own style. This new style was going to be demonstrated in this bout and everyone was holding their breath in anticipation.

The pair scrambled around at long range for a bit before Gotz finally darted in and behind Joe and went for a hammer lock and then a half-nelson. However, he wasn't able to get anywhere. Joe managed to shake the man off and slip behind Gotz and returned the favor by applying his own hammerlock. In response to this, Gotz employed his specialty, pulling Joe and flipping him over. Joe, however, had been champion for a decade and responded to this by deftly rolling away. This was a testament to his long years of experience. However, Gotz swooped in again like a bird of prey and wrapped up Joe from behind. He then lifted him up and was about to slam him on the ground. Joe, for his part, was not flustered, but hooked his right leg between Gotz's thighs and arched his body backwards with a grunt.

This caused Gotz, who was in the process of hoisting Joe up, to lose his balance, and with Joe's leg wrapped between his thighs, Gotz fell, flat on his back with Joe on top of him. The pair landed with a crash and both of Gotz's shoulders hit the mats at the same time signaling his defeat. Further, the impact of Joe's body on Gotz's solar plexus knocked him completely unconscious. Thus, Joe Carroll was declared the middle weight champion and he was awarded the Silver Cup. Gotz, as well as Henry, who had been beaten in an earlier match against Gotz that had lasted the full 30 minutes, were both eliminated from the tournament.

So as it turns out, in the lightweight division, it was Joe's nephew who was the champion and his uncle, Joe Carroll was the middle weight champion.

In the heavyweight division, all that remained for the final duels were Maeda and two others. Maeda would be taking on one of these two, and after Maeda was inevitably defeated, that man would be in the final with the third man. That meant one of the two men in the final would get the prize money for first place and the other would get the second place prize money.

Just as Maeda was glumly considering this, he got an unexpected stroke of luck. One of the men managing the fight? Apollo. Presented the following problem as well as a solution. "We are running short of time. I don't think we can fit in two more bouts. I say we make them in choose lots to eliminate one, then the other two will have a final duel."

Battle 33
Divine Grace and Throwing the Ozeki Ranked Wrestler

Much to Maeda's surprise, everyone agreed to Apollo's plan. After drawing lots, the man who was eliminated was James Morris Stockley, the champion from Manchester. The two remaining wrestlers were Maeda and the wrestler Jimmy Esson from Scotland. It was certainly bad luck for Stockley, since he had won every match up until now and was a favorite to take the first prize. At the very least, he would have certainly been favored to take second prize. At any rate, it was Maeda's lucky day as he was one of the two men in the final match. So even if Maeda lost this bout, he was still going to walk away with the second place prize. Maeda was determined to do his best and to make sure this was a spectacular duel. Now brimming with vim and vigor, Maeda felt nothing but love for the divine Apollo who had requested a drawing lots.

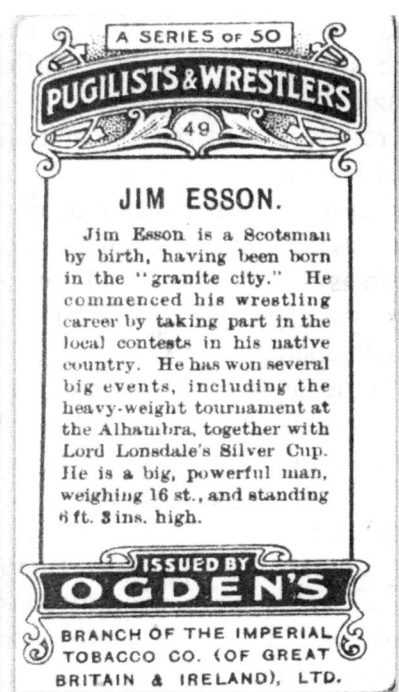

Jim Esson (1881~1917)

However, now that he looked carefully at his opponent, Maeda saw that Jimmy Esson was 6.4 Shaku tall and weighed close to 30 Kan.[48] If Maeda thought he might have one chance in ten of securing victory, he might have considered formulating some sort of plan of attack. But even after searching his mind from corner to corner, he couldn't find a path to victory. All he could think to do was to die gallantly in this battle.

From the very beginning of the match, the veteran warrior Esson was wary of even the smallest chance Maeda would throw him, so he held his giant body like the Japanese Hiragana letter 〈 Ku. He kept his arms, which were longer than Maeda's legs, extended out, meaning there was almost no chance of Maeda slipping behind him. If this were a sword fight, the size difference between opponents was like something out of a historical novel, like a duel between

---

[48] 192 centimeters/ 6 feet 4 inches. 113.5 Kilograms/ 248 pounds.

Wakaushimaru and Benkei. Even if Maeda was able to swoop down as fast as a bird of prey, he doubted he would be able to get past Esson's defenses. Since no one was wearing a Keikogi in this bout, it would simply be a contest of strength versus strength. That being said, Maeda wanted to get at least one good Ippon.[49]

Another surprising difficulty Maeda encountered as the match began was the fact that Esson did not seem inclined to go on the offensive. Thus, despite being a giant of a man, Esson was content to only edge forward carefully. This meant that Maeda couldn't use his opponent's power against him in a throw, so he decided to try and draw the man out. Maeda would advance and then immediately retreat in a different direction. When Esson moved in for a counter offensive Maeda would use his speed and small size to attack in some way. So, realizing that was all he had, Maeda leapt in at his opponent before darting quickly away. However, Esson made no move to follow, content to simply observe Maeda's actions. Soon the referee cautioned them, "Both of you need to be attacking!"

With that caution ringing in his ears, Maeda charged in and tried shoving Esson. Esson, for his part, had been keeping himself in reserve, and finally reacted to this attack like it was an insult and reached out with his long arms and seized Maeda's leg. Maeda, realizing he was in danger, yanked his leg free and dropped back. This time, Esson charged in after him. Maeda, who had just plucked the giants nose, met Esson with his go to technique Soto Muso, which is like Seoi Otoshi. The giant wasn't able to react in time, and before Esson could even shout, he was flying over Maeda's head. He landed with a crash on the mats and a huge cheer went up from the capacity crowd. With that throw Maeda had demonstrated his skill as a Judo practitioner and also what was possible with Judo. "That is something only a Judoka can do!" Shouted one gentleman in attendance.

For his part, Esson was wholly non-plussed by the throw, he simply rolled and stood up before dropping back down into his

---

[49] Referring to the warrior monk Saito Musashibo Benkei (1155~1189.) Benkei, who was a giant of a man, famously battled the much smaller Minamoto no Yoshitsune, who was known as Ushiwakamaru as a youth, and became his loyal servant after being defeated.

favorite stance, a ⟨ shape. Clearly, Maeda's throw hadn't affected him in the least. From the perspective of Judo, Maeda had scored a perfect Ippon, so for the rest of the match he was determined to throw himself directly at his opponent the moment he saw a gap in Esson's defenses.

Seeing one, Maeda leapt in close and slipped behind his opponent, wrapping him up from behind. Esson immediately dropped down onto all fours. Thus, despite the fact Maeda had succeeded in wrapping up Esson from behind, he didn't really have any way to attack his arms or neck because his enemy's body was so long Maeda's arms wouldn't reach. While Maeda was searching for a way to continue his attack, Esson grabbed both Maeda's wrists and with a mighty shake of his giant body, stood and threw Maeda off. No matter how hard Maeda had tried to hold on, he was sent flying. Maeda couldn't withstand one shake of the champion wrestler Esson's 6.4 Shaku 36 Kan body.[50]

So with one great movement, the giant Esson had ended Maeda's assault and now the pair were back glaring at each other. Maeda again attacked with wild abandon while leaping this way and that, Esson advanced and pushed on Maeda's neck. Maeda responded by dropping his hips and feinting like he was going for Esson's legs. Esson, thinking he was in danger, shoved Maeda's shoulders as he dropped back, thereby standing straight up in the process. Seeing an opening, Maeda drove in deep looking for a hips throw, but Esson was too quick, shooting his hips back. Maeda realized he wouldn't be able to get his hips in deep enough for a throw, so he switched to a Sutemi, sacrifice throw. Maeda swept Esson's left foot and shoved him backwards with all his might. Caught off guard, Esson dropped down onto his butt, but was able to hold himself there and, at the same time, Essen deftly shot out his left arm and grabbed Maeda's leg as he quickly rotated his body. Then, with his long right arm Essen seized Maeda about the waist.

If Maeda started thrashing around trying to escape, he would get pinned. So instead he dropped down onto all fours. Once Esson had Maeda on the ground, he began attacking with an unrelenting series of hammerlocks, half-nelsons and nelsons. Though Maeda tried to

---

[50] This is a different weight from before. 135 Kilograms/ 297 pounds

slip these attacks and escape, as soon as he got free, Esson's long arms soon roped him back in. While Maeda was able to deflect many attacks, he couldn't escape Esson's arms, which continued to try and wrap him up. Finally, the timekeeper shouted, "Thirty minutes!" And with that, the match was over. Maeda had lost.

Since this was the final of the tournament, it was the best two rounds out of three. So after a ten minute break, the second round began. Maeda can hardly be said to have recovered after the first round of battling a man twice his size, but he gave it his all, though everyone could see he was tired. He had no energy to bound around like he had done in the first round. That being said, Maeda had a fierce desire to get at least one more Ippon in this match, so Maeda prowled around the ring like a tiger, looking for an opportunity to strike when he found a gap in his opponent's defenses, he darted in and locked his body tight against his opponent and, burning through his last reserves of energy, threw his giant opponent. Esson was slammed down on his butt with a Seoi Otoshi-like technique called Soto Muso.

However, with that last effort Maeda reached his limit. Having achieved his goal, Maeda's exhaustion and lack of attention meant that he was slow in reacting when Esson slipped behind him and started applying a half-nelson to Maeda's exhausted body. Maeda was able to escape the lock once, however, the second time Esson's long right arm locked securely under Maeda's armpit and gripped the back of his neck like a vice, while his left hand locked around his waist. Esson hoisted Maeda up and since Maeda was small Esson was able to flip him onto his back without too much trouble and pinned Maeda's shoulders to the mats for the win.

Maeda had fought to within an inch of his life in this second round, which had lasted 14 minutes and 15 seconds. So Esson was crowned with the laurel wreath and received a silver cup filled with a thousand yen worth of coins. Maeda, thanks to the lottery system, had been awarded second prize to repay the ferocious efforts he had put forth day after day over the course of the difficult matches in this tournament. As it turned out, the crowd, having enjoyed seeing the two wrestlers of vastly different height and weight battle it out, were well satisfied with the performance given by Maeda. So it turned out they were all shouting his name, not Esson's despite the fact that Maeda had lost.

After the match, Maeda and Esson shook hands and the combatants started to walk off the stage. However, the sound of applause from the audience redoubled and the crowd began chanting Maeda's name. So Maeda turned around and went back out to thank the crowd again. However, as he turned to go a second time, the applause picked up again and he had to make a third appearance. Then a fourth. The last time, Esson wrapped his long arm over Maeda's shoulder like he was his son, and escorted him out in front of the crowd. Once there Maeda thanked them again before giving a willing Esson another hip toss, slamming him into the ground with a tremendous *boom!* The crowd erupted in cheers, and a man could be heard shouting, "Thank you for showing us how you can throw that big man!" There is a picture of Esson at the beginning of this book.[51]

Finally, there was the award ceremony, where the winners opened bottles of champagne and a grand time was had by all. The next day a motion picture newsreel of the final bout began showing and was very well received.[52] Maeda had no idea the match had been filmed, so he was startled when he heard about it. Going to see it, he saw a man a head shorter than his opponent, wrestling for all he was worth. Maeda could see how his brow had been covered with sweat. He could see how his Sarumata, monkey pants, were sagging around his short legs and his bread-colored skin looked nearly black in the motion picture. The film even showed him wiping the sweat from under his armpits and his opponent grabbing him up from behind, as well as the curious expression Maeda made while trying to wriggle free. All of this was recorded forever on film. "This film of

---

[51] "Famous Wrestler Killed. Every branch of British sport is represented in casualty lists published in England and issued from the Western Front. Jimmy Esson, the famous heavyweight wrestler who was captured, has died of wounds in Germany. Esson attained the rank of Sergeant Major. He won the heavyweight champion in The Catch as Catch Can tourney, held at the Alhambra, London in 1908, defeating the Jap Maida Yamato in the final by two straight falls."

-*Times of London*
1917

[52] One hopes this video can be located at some point.

our inter-discipline match is probably my greatest treasure from London." The motion picture was great fun and Maeda laughed as he watched it.

This all took place after New Year's 1908, up until the beginning of February 1908. Though Maeda lost, this was a no-gi "naked" Western-style wrestling match and Maeda had thrown his opponent Esson with Soto Muso twice so it was unquestionably a victory for Judo. Further, considering that Maeda had to fight naked it was also a win for him. [53]

Battle 34
Defeating an Opponent With One Blow[54]

A few days after the Alhambra tournament ended, Maeda got an invitation to duel. It was from the wild-Samurai middle weight Henry, who Maeda had previously defeated. Maeda was all for it, and their respective managers arranged the whole thing. Henry was managed by Brown, who ran the National Boxing Club in London, while Maeda was managed by Apollo.

The event ended up being held at the same site as the tournament, the Alhambra Theater. Maeda thought this would be a good chance to practice Western style wrestling. He wanted to show that he was a Judo practitioner that very much wanted to do Western style

---

[53] "On February 29 Maida Yamato and H. Irslinger, an Austrian wrestler, met in London in catch-as-catch-can style for ₤50 a side and a purse. It will be remembered that in the recent tournament Irslinger threw the Jap, but on February 29 Yamato won. The contest was to be decided by the best of three falls, but, as it happened, Yamato, after being thrown in 19min. 25sec., turned the tables on his opponent in the next bout, Irslinger hurting his shoulder so badly that he could not go on. The match was therefore awarded to Yamato."

-*The Australian Star*
Saturday, 11 April 1908

[54] The title of this chapter is Gaishu Issoku 鎧袖一触 defeating an armored opponent with one touch of his sleeve (forearm.) It refers to beating someone hands down or with a single mighty blow.

wrestling, so he didn't wear a Keikogi. It is important to note that the English make a distinction between the two martial arts, they feel that wrestling is wrestling and that Judo is Judo. So even if Maeda lost this wrestling match, it wouldn't besmirch, the name of Judo.

The contest would be best of three. At the start of the first round, Maeda attacked Henry with a variety of throws, but try as he might, he wasn't able to successfully translate his attacks to a pin. At some point, Henry locked up Maeda with a full nelson, much like Maeda had experienced during the tournament. However, despite this hold being forbidden, the referee didn't say anything, so Maeda had no choice but to wrench himself free by force.

He arched his back, but in the midst of this, Henry was able to pin his shoulders to the ground. Thereby winning the round. The total time was 19 minutes and 10 seconds. For the second round Maeda was determined not to allow himself to fall for that hold. Again, he concentrated on throwing Henry, hoping to wear the man out. Maeda thought that if he tired Henry enough he could finish him with another technique. So initially after throwing Henry, Maeda simply released and didn't try for a pin. Instead he waited for Henry to stand and engage again. After throwing Henry several times, Maeda could tell the man was tiring, so after the next throw he wrapped the man up from behind. However, Henry immediately dropped down onto all fours from that position. From there he could defend against Maeda's attacks while resting. The fact that Western wrestlers could rest in such a position was remarkable. For his part, Maeda didn't want to waste time struggling with his opponent in that position. "I need to throw him really hard, then immediately pin him!" Maeda thought. And with that he released his hold on Henry.

As soon as Maeda had let go, Henry stood. Not wasting any time, Maeda charged in close and wrapped his arms around Henry. Then, using all his strength, Maeda threw Henry with Ura Nage.

Caught off guard, Henry was slammed into the mats, striking his neck and shoulder. After a few moments passed, he turned to the referee and said, "I can't fight anymore" Thus Maeda was declared the victor.

Reflecting on his win, Maeda said. "When he was down on all fours, it was impossible for me to pin him. With respect to wrestling, he was the stronger fighter" Laughing, he added, "Of course, if this were a judo match, I would toss him around like a child."

Later, Henry paid a visit to the Dojo and asked Maeda if he would teach him some standing techniques. As it turned out, they were not able to arrange time to train, however, as Henry was young, strong and full of vim and vigor, Maeda felt that Judo training combined with the man's natural aggressiveness in the ring would mean the young man would have been able to reach Shodan level quickly.

The Powerful Woman Who Loved Judo

The result of advancing so far in the Western wrestling tournament as an outsider was that Maeda became well known in the wrestling community. The newspapers had also widely reported. Maeda's success. Thus he was receiving up to ten letters a day from acquaintances who lived in or around London. They were some variation of, "Congratulations on your victory" or "I'm writing to congratulate you on your victory the other day."

Many people also came by the Dojo to meet him. One day a woman in her fifties came with a letter of introduction. This aunty who lived in London was interested in restarting the Judo training after a hiatus. From the way she spoke to how she acted, the London Judo Auntie seemed like a man. She smoked cigarettes and after training she would sit cross legged with the men and remained even when the conversation turned rather coarse. In fact, the London aunty left the men with mouths agape at her bawdry stories. Judo Auntie was something Maeda had never encountered before.

The Judo Auntie had seen Maeda's performance at the Alhambra Theatre and had become a fan of the way Maeda had fought. She had decided to support Maeda with a surprising passion, as if he were her own child. She even wrote articles for the newspaper she was associated with, discussing Judo, Western wrestling and including Maeda's opinions on the subject. The Englishman at the Dojo all called her Judo-kyo, "Crazy about Judo," and there weren't any people that wrestled her seriously. While her clothes were female the patterns were masculine, so she had a curious appearance. Once she invited Maeda to a local pub. When she went in, she sat down on the bench taking up a lot of space, and proceeded to order first whiskey and then brandy. She chugged each of these down with a cheer of *Banzai!* Maeda was too startled to speak.

At some point, the Judo Auntie's talk shifted to volatile matters, and she launched into a scorching criticism of the political leadership of the day. Now in high spirits, she began talking about Buddhism. Apparently she was very interested in the subject of Buddhism in Japan. Next, she began encouraging Maeda to write a book about Judo. "The thing about Judo is that all that twisting the arms and twisting the neck isn't particularly valuable. The important thing is how Judo practice develops a person's mental abilities. It should be taught as if it's a religion. This is exactly what your Kano Sensei is talking about!"

Maeda was astonished that the Judo Auntie knew Kano Sensei's name.

At this point, the London Judo Auntie was more than a little tipsy and her opinions became even harsher. "These days all British people think about is betting money and they don't concern themselves at all with the development of with the psychological development of today's youth, which is going to destroy the UK from within!" Turning to Maeda, who was getting pretty deep into his cups himself, she offered an invitation.

"You really have been going nonstop over the past few weeks. Why don't we take a couple of days off and go and see Brighton"

Brighton was about a two and a half hour locomotive ride from London, where the city folk would go to escape the heat of summer or the cold of winter. It is much like Hakone in Japan. Maeda thought that it would be fun to do some sightseeing and they agreed to go the next day.

When he arrived at the station, he found that the London Judo Auntie had already purchased a train ticket for him. At Brighton, they checked into a hotel and had dinner, which the Judo Auntie insisted on paying for. After dinner, they retired to the smoking room where the Judo Auntie first lit a cigarette before summoning the waiter and ordering whiskey. The other customers were staring at her with grimaces on their faces, but the Judo Auntie paid them no mind. Maeda couldn't help but think the London Judo Auntie was another curious sort of person, much like the elderly gentleman from Kitman. That being said, the London Judo Auntie took that eccentricity to a whole another level.

The London auntie, who is crazy about Judo, had relatives who lived in Brighton. They apparently had a large house and the family were wealthy due to the fact that it had many investments. "If you have time tomorrow, you really must pay a visit!" the Judo Auntie said. Then she went off to her relatives house while Maeda stayed at the hotel.

For the next two days Maeda did some sightseeing and though he thought about visiting the London Auntie's house, since interacting with her was exhausting, in the end he went back to London. Through letters, the London Judo Auntie continued to encourage Maeda to write a book, but Maeda replied with, "I think I will wait until I am done with my training pilgrimage around the world." Later on the London Judo Aunty said, "I have to go a small town out in the countryside and help with girls' education, come and visit if you have time." However since Maeda remained busy, he never got around to visiting. Later he received a letter asking him to bring his Keikogi and visit her in the countryside for some training, but he wasn't able to get away.

I wonder what the London Judo aunty is up to now?

How Judo Got Started in the UK

The success of the wrestling match at Alhambra Theatre seemed to stimulate a great deal of renewed interest in wrestling in the UK with wrestling becoming popular all over again. Lancaster was probably the place in the United Kingdom, where wrestling was practiced with the most fervor. In that area, youth begin training at the age of eight or nine. The bouts are always held outside. The reason for this is, if they are held inside, it makes them seem as if they are fixed matches.

A group of dedicated Lancaster wrestlers even pooled their money to make a silver belt, which they presented it to any youth that wins the championship. Further, if the winner of the belt is able to defeat all subsequent challengers for the next six months he can then keep the belt forever.

It becomes the property of that champion.⁵⁵

Upon hearing about this tradition, Maeda was immediately overwhelmed with an intense desire to challenge the owner of such a belt so that he could send it back to Japan as a souvenir. So he asked around to see if anyone knew a person who possessed such a belt. Unfortunately, while he was able to locate a man that had such a belt, he was the lightweight champion. The wrestler was a small fellow weighing only 110 Kin, 66 kgs/ 145 pounds. Since Maeda weighed 150 Kin, 90 kgs/ 198 pounds, even if he fasted, he wouldn't be able to get down to 110 Kin. Frustrated, he turned to the smallest of his friends and said, "Can I get you to wrestle that guy and then give me the belt?"

However, the man replied, "That sounds like a job for Yukio." Referring to the Japanese man who have been living in London for close to a decade. Yukio was a veteran wrestler who had trained extensively in Western-style wrestling.

At this point it is probably necessary, as well as likely interesting, to take the time to talk about who the first Japanese Judoka in the UK was and what methods he used to introduce Judo in this foreign land. About fifteen or sixteen years ago, a British train engineer travelled to Japan. Upon his return, he hired two Japanese Judoka to accompany him back to London and teach Judo.⁵⁶ The first is a man we all consider to be our elder brother is Tani Yukio, who still lives

---

⁵⁵

First Official British Catch-as-catch-can Championship Belt, 1899
Winner: Joe Carroll of Hindley, Lancs

⁵⁶ In 1900, the nineteen-year old Yukio, his brother Kaneo and a fellow Jujutsuka Yamamoto Seizo (?-?) travelled to London by invitation of Edward William Barton-Wright, the founder of Bartitsu.

in London. The other is a man named Yamamoto Seizo who is a Judoka that lives in Osaka. This Yamamoto was originally a disciple of Handa[57] but later became a member of the Kodokan. This was more or less around the time Maeda became Shodan.

In Meiji 31 (1898,) about fourteen years ago, Yamamoto was considered to be the top wrestler in Osaka and indeed the whole Kansai area. At this time, Nagaoka Rokudan, who was a Kodokan Yondan at the time, dominated all the wrestlers in the area, both inside the Kodokan and out.[58] He happened to be in Kyoto at the Butokukai and he had a bout with Yamamoto.

Nagaoka used Yoko Sutemi, on both the left and right sides, to throw Yamamoto and win. With that victory, the name of Nagaoka came to dominate the Kansai, Judo and Jujutsu scene. Yamamoto was a "big soldier" who weighed 27 Kan, 101 kgs/ 223 lbs. He along with Ueno Nidan were known as the giants of eastern and western Japan.[59]

Before leaving for the UK, Yamamoto paid a visit to the Kodokan and met with Yokoyama Nanadan and joined the Kodokan. At that point, Maeda had just risen to Nidan and was practically crackling with energy. He was ordered to wrestle Yamamoto, the new member. Seated in the Yudansha [60] section were Yokoyama Nanadan, Nagaoka Rokudan and other of the original members, now in their middle years. It was quite a scene. If Maeda had been facing off with a long standing member, the bout would have been nothing to comment on, however this bout felt like he was going up against a member of another school of Jujitsu. Maeda felt that this was a bigger match even than the annual Red versus White tournament held at the Kodokan. Yamamoto, for his part, had already made a name for himself in another school of Jujitsu, likely considered this

---

[57] Handa Yataro 半田彌太郎（1847-1912）Founder of 大東流柔術 Daito Ryu Jujutsu.

[58] Nagaoka Shuichi 永岡秀一 (1876 ~1952) An member of the Kodokan and the third person to be promoted to 10th dan. "Rokudan" is sixth-degree black belt.

[59] Ueno Magokichi 上野孫吉

[60] Yudansha are Judoka who have achieved at least Shodan, first degree black belt and above.

duel nothing more than regular training. However, Maeda, who had just advanced in rank and was full of vim and vigor, was determined to fight with every ounce of his being.

In this duel, Maeda was able to throw Yamamoto several times. Despite the fact that the big fat "soldier" was 10 Kan, 38 kgs/ 82 lbs. heavier than Maeda, he was able to throw him four or five times using Tsuri Komi Goshi. Maeda had the following to say about the duel,

"Of all the duels I had in Japan. That one is by far the most memorable. I had just been awarded Nidan and I was as energetic as the rising sun. While there were other big guys in the Kodokan like Ono, here weren't any giants like Yamamoto who weighed 27 Kan, 101 kgs/ 223 lbs. Remembering the way the ground reverberated as I slammed his giant body down with Tsuri Komi Koshi still brings a smile to my face. That day several other Yudansha, not including Nagaoka Rokudan, wanted to take a turn dueling the new member. Yamazaki Sandan[61] took on Yamamoto but he wasn't able to land a single Ippon."

"I thought that if I took on Yamazaki Sandan he would lose. In short, I felt more joy after that win than I did after winning all my bouts in Shinkyu Shobu, dueling any opponents in succession in order to advance in rank. I have no doubt I'm looking at the past through rose colored glasses, but I clearly remember how that match went and how I used my best technique to win it."

Thus Maeda was well acquainted with one of the pair that first introduced Judo in London. However, as it turned out a few months after Yamamoto and Tani had travelled to the UK, their contract for teaching was abruptly abandoned. Instead, the pair were pressured into engaging in public duels. They complained that this was not part of their contract, however, negotiations didn't go anywhere and eventually their one year contract was up, so they left the UK and returned to Japan.

Later, elder-brother Tani returned to London. However, instead of Yamamoto, he came with a Judoka from Osaka named Kaminishi

---

[61] Yamazaki Wataru (?) 山崎亘 (?~?)

Sadakazu.⁶² They have been running a Judo Dojo here ever since. However, as it turned out, while the Judo club was initially very successful and had many students, the club eventually became insolvent. Tani and Kaminishi decided to quit working for the club and go independent. However, due to a combination of their lack of English ability, along with the fact that Judo wasn't as well known then as it is now, they soon found their business was floundering. It was at this point the god of good fortune, Apollo, appeared. Apollo was an expert at making a plan of action and he assured the pair that if he managed them they would surely succeed, so Tani signed a three-year contract with Apollo.

Apollo's vision was, "To have Tani duel with well-known wrestlers and show how Judo can win. In short, to raise the profile of Judo."

Tani agreed to this proposal, and they found a lightweight champion who was about the same size as Tani. His name was Jimmy and he was a "small soldier" catch wrestling champion. Before engaging in this match, Tani had trained Western style wrestling for several months. For the actual match, Tani didn't use Judo and he also didn't wear a Keikogi. In short, it was a Western style "naked" wrestling match. The match ended in a dispute, so the pair did the match over. In the end, Tani handily defeated his opponent. With that, Tani leaped to fame with this unexpected victory. Seizing on this opportunity, Apollo announced Tani's next bout would be a Judo match. Apollo sent out the following challenge to papers all over the UK, "Anyone who wishes to take on Tani is welcome. The challenger can use whatever techniques he so chooses. Any fighter who is victorious will receive a cash reward!"

This is how Tani and Japanese Judo became widely known in the UK, then after Japan's victory in the Russo-Japanese War the topic of Judo became so popular that people even went so far as to say, "I am not interested in talking to a person who doesn't know anything about Japanese Judo."

---

⁶² Uyenishi Sadakazu 上西貞一 (1880~?) Who also used the name Raku while in London. He is credited with introducing Jujitsu to the British army and police. His dojo was called the *School of Japanese Self Defense*

In fact, Judo was so popular that even the wives of the gentry began to take lessons. As for Kaminishi at one point he returned to Japan, but then later returned to the UK along with another Judoka named Miyake Taruji.[63] They sought to play off the success Tani was having. However, due to various circumstances, Miyake ended up joining Tani and this left Kaminishi out in the cold.

Miyake was a big man and more than a match for money or community. Tani and Miyake had a duel one time but Tani lost five out of 6 bouts. Interestingly, the English didn't consider this to be a loss for Tani. Up until now Tani had been a household name to the point that if the subject, of Judo, came up, people would invariably mention Tani.

Further, if an Englishman went abroad and met another Japanese Judoka, he would comment something along the lines of, "In our country we have Tani!" as if he were a citizen of the UK. This is because Tani was the first man to defeat a well-known Western wrestler. He was then the first to embark on a journey around the UK issuing challenges as a Judoka. Foreigners are of the opinion that much like their wrestling, Judo required opponents to be the same weight, so a duel between two fighters of unequal weights was not really a fair duel. Thus, even though Miyake soundly defeated Tani, the citizens of the UK simply brushed it off, "With big a weight difference, it hardly can be considered a loss!"

In other words, the British view Judo much like their own native Wrestling tradition. If there was a weight imbalance between opponents, then even if the lighter person lost, it doesn't count against them. At present Ono Sandan is in London, however he doesn't draw much attention. He weighs 24 or 25 Kan, 90~94 kgs/ 198~207 lbs, but since the English are all already familiar with how the 14 ~15 Kan, 53~56 kgs/ 116~124 lbs "small soldier" Tani wrestles, even if he lost to Ono, they would wave it aside and say, "With that big a size difference, you wouldn't even have to know Judo to twist Tani into a pretzel." The reason they believe this is because a typical duel won't have kicks or Atemi, strikes to vital areas, because they consider such attacks dangerous.

Tani was formerly a police officer and received his Shodan after training with Yamashita Nanadan. Later he traveled to the UK

---

[63] Taro Miyake (c. 1881~1935)

where he had many trials and tribulations which forced him to refine his techniques. Now he was a skilled veteran, and is able to use his experience to achieve victories that would seem beyond his level on paper. The reason Judo is flourishing in the UK is due to Tani's many difficult fights and Apollo's careful managements. Thus, despite the fact that Ono and Miyake were the better Judoka. They respected the territory Tani had roped off and sought to find their own way in the UK.

The Battle for the Silver Belt

After that introduction, let us return to the competition over the silver belt. It appeared the only way to get a hold of one was for Tani to be the one to challenge the holder. Tani agreed to the plan and Maeda would accompany him to assist. They headed to a coal mining town called Oldham, which was just outside Manchester City. At the time the Silver championship belt was held by a "small soldier" named Willie Collins.[64] Unfortunately, when they arrived in Oldham they found another challenger had already applied for a fight. Thus Tani couldn't directly challenge Collins he had to first dual a man named Bobby[65] who applied first in order to have a chance at winning the belt.

When Maeda and Tani set out for Oldham it was February of Meiji 41, the coldest time of year.

As was mentioned before, in this area, they wrestle shirtless outdoors. Maeda was serving as Tani's corner man and so he was wearing a heavy coat with a scarf wrapped around his neck. Despite this, it was so cold Maeda was shivering as he watched the match which was taking place in the middle of a field, with the cold wind howling out of the north. Further, since early that morning, dark, suspicious looking clouds had been covering the sky and now, as the match began, the clouds began to drop white, powdery snow. This made the place seem even colder.

Despite these poor conditions, the match wasn't called off and both combatants stripped naked and did the weigh-in. If the two were not of equivalent weight, then the match would probably be

---

[64] Unknown.
[65] Possibly Bob Berry (?~?).

called off. Tani had been a bit heavier than his opponent, so two or three days before the match, he reduced his meal portions and went to Turkish baths. He reduced his weight until he was within half a Kin of his opponent's weight.[66]

After the weigh-in was finished, the two combatants finally shook hands and began. The moment the two locked up, the wind picked up and snow began to fall in earnest, Maeda recalled, "Even now I can recall how fearfully cold it was there, watching in the swirling snow." At first, the two brave warriors moved vigorously, however, soon their lips began to turn blue and they stopped being able to bend their fingers. Even the spectators found the cold hard to bear. Though the spectators shouted enthusiastically, the match continued without a resolution. Tani, for his part, was attacking from the very beginning, however, his opponents defenses were very strong. It seemed as if this match continued from much longer both combatants would freeze to death. Tani, however, who was clearly in the lead had no desire to call for an end to the bout. If he did so, he would have to endure a thousand blind people scoffing that Japanese can't handle the cold.[67]

Then Bobby, who was under Tani at this time called out, "It's too cold. I can't go on!" Thus the 45 minute duel ended in a draw, with both combatants promising to resume the match on the following day.

After a draw was declared, the two competitors suddenly began shivering violently and people came forward to wrap them in warm clothing and seat them in chairs. They were so cold they couldn't even talk. Before the match, Maeda had heard murmuring of, "While Tani may be the better wrestler, he won't be able to take this cold and it will lead to his defeat" However, as it turned out, it was Bobby who requested the match be halted, and when the pair stood up, he clearly looked as if the cold had gotten the worst of him.

Maeda commented, "His lips were purple and he was shaking so hard he couldn't speak. His whole body was cold as ice. It is too bad he stood in the way of Tani earning the silver belt! Even today

---

[66] Kin 斤 1 Kin is about .6 kilograms or 1.3 pounds.

[67] 盲千人目明き千人 is a proverb, *some are wise and some are otherwise; one thousand blind; one thousand with their eyes open*

thinking of how that man's eyes were darting around in a panic over how cold he was makes me smile." While both men had fought valiantly, it was time to let them retire for now. Maeda and Tani took the rest of the day off before returning to London.

Unfortunately they were not able to reschedule the match and before they knew it the six month time limit had passed and they lost their chance to claim the belt.

MAEDA MITSUYO : UK 1907 ~ 1908

A Tough Fight for Ono Sandan

Not long after, with the excitement of the Alhambra tournament still in the air, another wrestling tournament began. This time it was held at Hengler's Circus.[68] The tournament would feature over two hundred wrestlers divided into three classes: Heavyweight, Middleweight and Lightweight. The winner of the heavyweight division would get £100 pounds, equivalent to ¥1000. The

---

[68] "The big wrestling tournament, catch-as-catch-can-style, at the Alhambra Music-hall, has proved a great success, a very large number of good men of all weights and dimensions having taken part in it. After lasting several days and furnishing some fine sport, the end came on Monday in the decisive triumphs for British wrestlers over the many foreigners who took part. Joe Carroll, of Hindley, won the middle-weights, beating the somewhat famous Peter Gotz (11st. 4lb. champion) in the final; Jack Carroll (nephew of "Joe ") taking the light-weights; and James Esson, of Aberdeen, securing the heavy-weights. Esson, who is only 22 years of age, stands 6ft. 3 3/4in., weighs in condition 16st., and is immensely powerful. His opponent in the final was an extremely clever little "Jap," Maido Yamato (Maeda used this name in the UK), who was, however, at a great disadvantage, being only 5ft. 6 1/2in. in height and 11st. 4lb. in weight. The chief prizes in the three divisions were respectively £25, £50, and £80—with a valuable cup in every class, added by Lord Lonsdale.

An even better-class tourney, but in the Greco-Roman style, is now in progress at Hengler's Circus, several first-class men taking part in it, and the money prizes being far more valuable. The winner—of course, in this style there is only one class—will take £200, second £100, third £80, fourth £50, and so on. This tourney is being engineered by M. Beketour, proprietor of the circus, and will last a considerable time, judging by the great array of foreign and home talent entered for it."

-SPORTING NOTES FROM HOME
By Robin Hood
February 7th 1908

middleweight winner would get £50, or ¥500 and the lightweight division would get £25, or ¥250. There were no prizes for second or third place, however if wrestlers were deemed sufficiently skilled, their room and board for the whole week was paid. This was part of the manager's plan from the outset and was quite different from how the athletes were handled at the Alhambra Theater event. Thus, a lot of bets were being made since most of the athletes were wrestlers by trade.

Maeda had decided not to enter the tournament since he wasn't associated with any of the wrestling organizations associated with the event. He felt entering the contest would be like jumping in out of the blue. If he did join it might be disrespectful to try and sort out what was going on after he had entered the ring. Add to the fact that Maeda had performed admirably in the Alhambra Tournament so he decided he wouldn't enter this tournament. However, Apollo wouldn't hear of it, "You don't have to worry about being an outsider. Trust me on this, no matter what happens on the mats it won't adversely affect Judo's reputation."

Thus, in the end, Maeda entered the tournament and he racked up win after win for the first five days. Unfortunately, on sixth day he was forced to withdraw, after coming down with a bad cold. An unfortunate turn of events and things didn't go in his favor and they had at the Alhambra tournament.

Ono Sandan also participated in this tournament as well, battling in the heavyweight division. Maeda thought that with a little bit of training in Western style wrestling, Ono could probably emerge as champion, particularly if he stayed on the offensive. However, Ono wasn't interested in training, therefore, since he was not the type to charge in attacking ferociously, he was knocked out on the third day.

Ono's opponent was Jimmy Lemm of Sweden (sic. Switzerland) who beat Ono in four minutes flat. While Ono could still continue to compete in the tournament, only those who had remained undefeated could compete in the final. A very unfortunate end to the tournament. The man Ono wrestled, Jimmy Lemm, was shorter and lighter in weight than Ono, but was absolutely bulging with muscles. Lemm was extremely strong. While foreign wrestlers tend to have weak hips, Lemm was like a rock with powerful hips and legs.

John (Johann) Lemm
(1883~1961)

Ono Akitaro 大野秋太郎
(?~1928?)
An exemplar of Kodokan Judo
April 1908

Lemm preferred to remain standing and employ various throws rather than drop down on all fours and grapple on the ground. When Lemm locked up with Ono Sandan, he tried two or three times to throw Ono by the neck. Ono Sandan, for his part, tried to wrench Lemm around but was instead shoved to the ground in a surprising turn of events.

Looking from the sidelines, Maeda could only shake his head and disbelief, "Why didn't Ono use that chance to throw with Ura Nage!?" The whole match was very frustrating for him to watch. "How come whenever I'm in the ring I never get an opponent that likes? Standing techniques like that, they always end up. Squaring off against Ono." Maeda complained.

The tournament lasted a month, and the heavyweight champion was the man, Lemm, who beat Ono. The middle weight division champion was Henry, who Maeda knocked unconscious with an Ura Nage at the previous Alhambra Tournament. The lightweight winner was Oel Collins Who was the man Velly had challenged, hoping to snatch the silver belt from. Later, Maeda was able to arrange a Judo duel with Jimmy Lemm and submitted the man in less than four minutes. There is a picture of him at the beginning of this book.

After the tournament at Hengler's Circus ended, many of the previously introduced wrestlers would move on to Manchester for another event. There was also a large contingent of contingent of warriors headed to a tournament in Glasgow.[69]

---

[69] "A surprising result followed a wrestling match at Hengler's Circus, London, for £100 between the Turk, Pengal, and a Japanese wrestler named Diabutsu. The former had undertaken to throw the Jap three times in an hour, or forfeit £100. If Diabutsu gained even one fall in the time stated the money was to go to him. On the men getting together Pengal did most of the attacking, but after 13 min. 30 sec. of strenuous work, Diabutsu rolled him over on his back, and secured the £100."

-Cairns Morning Post
Thursday 30 April 1908

Submitting the Russian Lion

Immediately following the tournament at Hengler's Circus another tournament began at a theatre on Oxford Street, London's equivalent of Ginza Street. The world champion catch wrestler Hackenschmidt, known as the Russian Lion, was holding a week-long event there. The event was extremely popular with many people attending as if it were the final day of a Sumo tournament in Japan. Everyone seemed to be talking about it.

One morning, Maeda saw a newspaper article by Hackenschmidt in the morning paper. At the end of the article contained the following paragraph,

I really don't hear much about Japanese Judo anymore, despite the fact it made a big splash and got a lot of people talking. No doubt because European wrestling has swept it off the map, it seems it was just a flash in the pan so we wrestlers don't pay attention when anyone talks about Judo training.

Maeda got up, shoved the newspaper into the breast pocket of his jacket and charged over to the theater on Oxford Street by himself. "He's Hackenschmidt here?" He demanded, and someone told him the wrestler was talking with his manager about tonight's fight in the prep room. However, when Maeda arrived, he found that Smith[70] had gone to the dressing room. So Maeda charged up the stairs to the second floor and finally found Smith.

Maeda shoved the newspaper in Smith's face and began to berate the man in his rather dubious English regarding the contents of the article. Whether or not Smith understood is debatable, but the gist of it was, "I can't believe someone who is considered to be the world wrestling champion would talk about Judo in such an irresponsible manner. Right here and right now, let's decide the good and bad points about Judo and Western wrestling. A debate can go on forever, so instead of arguing whose field should be watered in the middle of a drought, let's wrestle here and now. There are already mats on the ground!"

Stunned by Maeda's sudden entrance and subsequent

---

[70] Maeda calls Hackenschmidt "Smith" for the rest of the book.

confrontation, the world wrestling champion, the Lion of Russia, seemed unable to respond. He just stood there at first and seemed only to be able to open and close his mouth, but no sound came out.

Maeda readied himself in the center of the space and declared, "At any rate, let's get down to brass tacks and have it out right here! If you can defeat me, write whatever insults about Judo that you want, including how inferior it is to Western wrestling. In Japan my abilities are considered to be almost off the scale, but I now find myself abroad trying to show foreigners what Judo is all about. I mean no offense to the other Japanese Judoka when I say this, but frankly, in the United Kingdom, there is no one more skilled than me at this art. Thus, if Western wrestlers wish to test their mettle against the top Judoka, then I am the man you are looking for. If I am unable to deliver a respectable performance, then feel free to say that Judo does not stand up to Western wrestling. So, you come at me with wrestling and I will go at you with Judo. We will have a duel with each of us doing our own style of fighting!" Maeda said this while glaring up at the man who stood a head taller.

In response to this Smith, the lion, seems taken aback and mumbled and excuse, completely devoid of any sort of confrontational tone, "I didn't say any of what is written in this article. The reporter must have added it."

However, Maeda didn't let Smith slither away from his responsibility and said, "You are the champion, and by attaching your name to this article, you are giving it credence. Do you want to be seen as a swindler or a fake champion? To top it all off, here I am in front of you showing you the words printed in your name and you are trying to prevaricate in a cowardly manner!?"

Despite this ferocious assaults, Mr. Lion didn't seem to have a lot to say, replying only with, "I didn't say any of this. I will immediately call the newspaper reporter I talked to yesterday and get this sorted out.

Maeda, who was unrelenting in his pressure said, "Very well. Then call him right now." So Smith called the reporter and about twenty minutes later the man appeared. Smith didn't bring the reporter into the room with Maeda and instead ushered him into the adjoining room. Presumably, Smith was attempting to get the man to accept all the blame for this situation.

Eventually the pair emerged and the reporter faced Maeda saying

"This error occurred due to my negligence and I offer my unreserved apologies. Mr. Smith is in no way associated with the remarks made about Judo, those were all written by me."
"What are you going to do about it?" Maeda responded.
"The paper will issue a retraction in the morning edition." The reporter said.

Since Maeda wasn't a gangster, he did the gentlemanly thing and let the matter rest. The reporter had promised that the paper would issue a full retraction of Smith's statement about Judo, so Maeda considered that aspect of the situation to be resolved. However, Maeda was looking for an opportunity to throw the world champion himself to prove he could handle wrestlers like children. Maeda was even thinking of showing off some techniques that had nothing to do with self-defense.

Maeda turned to Smith and made his offer, "While the retraction of the article has been settled, there really isn't anything preventing this reporter from slipping up again. So to prevent that, I think we should have a duel with this reporter as our witness. As I said before, you come at me with Western style wrestling and I will use Judo. We will both fight until one of us gives up."

However, Smith didn't respond, so Maeda tried another approach "Well another way we can do this is for me to strip naked and wrestle with you for thirty minutes Western style and then we will do thirty minutes in Judo style. That way the contest will be fair. Whichever person finishes fastest will be declared the winner. However, since Smith had seen the very strong performance Maeda had put in wrestling "naked" at Alhambra Theatre, he turned the offer down, saying, "I have never said anything bad about true Judoka. I think Judo is an unrivaled style of fighting, but as you know, I'm a Western style wrestler. Even though Judo is a completely different style, if I did enter a bout with you and then got thrown, it would affect my career. If I am defeated, even by another school of fighting, people around the world will only focus on the fact that I was beaten and say, "Smith was beaten, so he is not really the world champion anymore."

By the end of it, it almost sounded as if the lion were pleading with Maeda. Maeda made one last attempt. "That is why we will do thirty minutes of your style and thirty minutes of my style!" However, Smith declined saying, "No, I will never be able to defeat you in wrestling faster than you could defeat me in Judo. I don't see us as adversaries because wrestling is wrestling and Judo is Judo And we are both flourishing in our respective styles." And Smith finished quite humbly with, "That is why I do not presume to say this or that about Judo"

Maeda's plan had actually been to goad Smith into a fight by making him angry. However, Maeda seemed unable to provoke Smith.

Later, Maeda would frequently send challenge notices to the newspaper asking for a bout with Smith, offering a guarantee of ¥1000 prize. The match would be divided in half, with each of them wrestling half in their own style and half in the other style. But Smith never responded. The Great Lion did not act like a lion at all and instead seemed to have been cowed into silence.

So it seems that without fighting, Maeda was able to completely overcome the world champion. Interestingly the American Frank Gotch, who wrestled the champion Hackenschmidt was actually beaten by a compatriot of Maeda's named Itoh Yondan.[71] This was probably a Judo match. This means that both the American and European champions were completely flattened by Japanese Judoka. This just leaves the boxing champion, who is a black man. Thus the championship of the world will be a battle between a black fighter and a yellow fighter, with the white fighters having been left by the wayside.

It's well known that the Sumo wrestler Hitachi, who had departed London last year, sent all his boxing gear back to Japan and he told Maeda, "I've taken responsibility for tangling with boxers. I will leave the Western style wrestlers up to you lot." He and his students went to America unannounced, seeking to find a way to meet and crush Johnson.[72]

Hackenschmidt was about the same size as Ono Sandan, but since he was a world champion, he no doubt possessed considerable strength. Though he was from Russia, he had spent a long time in the UK and had many English backers. Last year he traveled to the US to fight the American champion Frank Gotch in Chicago. The

---

[71] Itoh Tokugoro 伊藤徳五郎 (?~?)

[72] Jack Johnson (1878~1946)

match went on for two hours before Hackenschmidt called for a stop. After that, Gotch claimed that he was in fact now the world champion. However, the reason Hackenschmidt called for a stop was because of Gotch's wild attacks. Hackenschmidt claimed that Gotch stuck his fingers in his eyes and nose in addition to biting him, in a fine example of how in America wrestlers will resort to dirty tricks in order to win. All over America, you see this type of cowardly behavior buried deep.

On April 3rd 1908 in Chicago, Frank A. Gotch (1877~1917) defeated George Hackenschmidt (1878~1968) the "Russian Lion" in an international wrestling match for the champion of the world.

While amongst the upper classes in America many fine examples of gentlemanly behavior can be found however, the other side of the coin are those attempting to expel all the immigrants and threatening some sort of stupid war between the US and Japan.[73] To add insult to injury, both the umpire as well as the police officer in charge of such fights have been paid off. The newspaper in the in the UK supported Smith unconditionally and were all critical of the American side and accused them of illegality. Upon Smith's return, the locals all cheered him and held a consolation party for him, even going so far as to collecting money for him and donate it to him.

There are pictures of Hackenschmidt at the beginning of this book.

The State of Sumo Wrestling in Europe

So the title "world champion" is a bit confusing in the West. The title, "Japan's top fighter," or "the best fighter in the world" can be misleading. For example, Hackenschmidt the man known as the Russian Lion is the world champion. So you would think that amongst all the wrestlers in the world, there would be none that were his equal. However, since there are always people aiming up, a Turkish man arrived in London looking to challenge the world champion. He was 6 Shaku and 5 or 6 Sun, 197~200 cm/ 6'5"~6'6" tall. The Turkish man made several attempts to contact Smith about a duel but was never able to get an agreement.

The word on the street was that Smith realized he wouldn't be able to take down the Turkish wrestler, probably because he knew he would have to relinquish his championship title. Maeda was able to find out where this Turkish wrestler was in London and went for a look. He saw that he was indeed 6.5 Shaku tall and Maeda

---

[73] The Gentlemen's Agreement of 1907 (日米紳士協約, Nichibei Shinshi Kyōyaku) was an informal agreement between the United States of America and the Empire of Japan whereby Japan would not allow further emigration to the United States and the United States would not impose restrictions on Japanese immigrants already present in the country. The goal was to reduce tensions between the two Pacific nations such as those that followed the Pacific Coast race riots of 1907 and the segregation of Japanese students in public schools. The agreement was not a treaty and so was not voted on by the United States Congress.

estimated the man weighted about weighed 40 Kan, 150 kg / 330 lbs. No doubt a man of that size would be able to pin Smith in less than five minutes.

While Smith was certainly strong he only weighs 24~25 Kan, 90 kg/ 198 lbs., and stands about 5 Shaku 6 Sun, 170 cm/ 5'6." If he agreed to a Judo bout, Maeda would have no problem throwing such a big man, however in Western style wrestling if there is a 1 Kan 3.75 kgs/ 8.3 lbs. difference in weight between the combatants, then the match is called off.

It seems that since Smith let himself be intimidated by this 40 Kan Turkish wrestler he should change his name to the Russian Lion Cub. Not exactly behavior becoming the world wrestling champion. This was still in Meiji 41 (1908) and the top Catch wrestlers were the American Frank Gotch and the Russian Hackenschmidt. As for the champions of Greco-Roman style wrestling there are the previously mentioned athletes, the Polish wrestler Stanislaus Zbysko, the Russian wrestler Ivan Poddubny, the French wrestlers Paul Ponce and Jess Peterson and the Italian wrestler Rese Eugene.

All of these men are considered to be a world champion. Also there are many considered to be champion in the boxing world. Recently, Jeffrey was defeated by the black fighter Johnson and he became the world champion.[74] However, in the middle weight and lightweight wrestling divisions, no one knows who the world champion is.

---

[74] The champion James Jeffries refused to face Jack Johnson (1878 ~1946) and retired instead. Johnson then pursued the Canadian champion Tommy Burns for nearly two years until Burns agreed to a bout. They fought on December 26, 1908, in Sydney and after fourteen rounds Johnson declared the winner. Later, Jeffries came out of retirement to challenge Johnson in 1910 and was beaten by Johnson.

This book was published in 1912 so it is not clear if the authors were confusing Jeffries and Burns or were referring to when Johnson beat Jeffries in 1910.

As far as name recognition goes, the Frenchman Ponce well as the Russian Hackenschmidt are the most famous. [75] The Turkish wrestler was almost totally unknown.

---

[75] George Hackenschmidt mentions Maeda in his book *Complete Science Of Wrestling*,

"Take the Alhambra tournament in 1908, and the progress of the little Jap, Yamato, into the final for the heavy-weight championship. Yamato was seemingly hopelessly outweighted in every bout; his stature was positively diminutive when contrasted with any of his antagonists, and ridiculously so when he faces such giants as Zipps and Esson.

Yet these opponents were obviously on thorns whenever they were called upon to face him in an upright posture, one of them even, although some five or six stones the heavier man, positively preferring to remain on his hands and knees, without making any attempt to rise, rather than run the risk of being again tripped and brought down heavily, as he had invariably been whenever he found his feet.

The two giants were seemingly confident that their tiny antagonist did not possess the necessary strength to lever over their own huge bulk, and were further dismally aware that this same bulk rendered their constant impact with the ground whenever Yamato tripped them decidedly unpleasant.

I have been told that the respect which these big fellows displayed for Yamato's legs was positively ludicrous. They never themselves presumed to take the liberty of attempting to trip him; yet, despite the fact that they bent themselves double in their precautions, and skipped away at every movement made by the Jap, they were unable to escape frequent violent visits to the mat."

- George Hackenschmidt
Complete Science Of Wrestling
2nd edition / revised by Percy Longhurst.
London : Athletic Publications, 1909

Hitachiyama Taniemon 常陸山谷右衛門(1874 ~ 1922)
Born Ichige Tani 市毛谷

The Sumo Wrestler Hitachiyama Threatens All of the UK

Backing up a bit, the champion Sumo wrestler Hitachiyama traveled first to America before coming over to London. After his demonstrations in the US were finished, Hitachi had sent his students back to Japan before travelling to London alone. His plan was to do some sightseeing before taking the Trans-Siberian Railroad back home. When he first arrived in America, he was invited to the White House to demonstrate Sumo to President Roosevelt. First, he did Dohyo Iri, the ceremonial opening of a Sumo match, and then continued on and showed typical Sumo training. Following his demonstration in front of the president, he did some presentations at a couple of colleges. However, Hitachiyama felt that the Americans didn't really seem all that impressed, Maeda, speaking from experience, said, "In the United States, doing an exhibition in front of the President doesn't grant you the same prestige as doing an exhibition in the presence of the Emperor. The best way to introduce your art is to rent a theatre and invite the general public. Offer prize money to anyone that wants to challenge you on the spot. You should have come to the UK first and demonstrated before the royal family and then rented a theatre and taken all comers." Maeda added, "It is a shame you didn't come to London before going to the US!"

While in London Hitachi was dressed like a gentleman as he went sightseeing. He had sent all his Sumo gear back to Japan and, because his "uncle" the man that helped him prepare his hair and garments had come down with a serious illness, Hitachi had encouraged him to return home to Japan as well. Thus, Hitachi wasn't prepared to put on a full Sumo display in London.

At around this time there was a big tournament going on in London and Zbysko, Poddubny and others were locked in competition.

Maeda turned to Hitachi and said, "You should enter the tournament and whip them all. Then you can return home wearing the laurel wreath of a world wrestling champion!" However Hitachi replied, "If we were dueling in Sumo, I could throw them around like rag dolls. However, trying to wrestle them in their own style would be hard going." Maeda was forced to agree with that assessment. Hitachi's giant fat body was perfect for shoving and throwing opponents while standing. Thus, while he was unparalleled in a standing duel, when the fight went down to the mats and both opponents were on all fours battling like dogs Hitachi would be in big trouble. Hitachi turned to Maeda and said, "I tried a little bit of Greco-Roman wrestling when I was in the US."

Japanese Sumo wrestlers put on weight, so their bellies are big, but this is not done in the West. Western wrestlers are very careful about what they eat, while Japanese Sumo wrestlers use their stomachs as giant battering ram to attack with. On the other hand if a Sumo wrestler does Western style wrestling and ends up on the ground, that same belly won't allow them to continue battling for an hour or two.

When Westerners see the fat wobbling bellies of Japanese Sumo wrestlers they tend to laugh out loud. The most extreme response to seeing a Sumo wrestler's big belly and top knot is, "That's a woman! I bet she can do night wrestling!"

Once, upon hearing this, Maeda couldn't take it anymore and retorted, "That is a stupid thing to say! Why don't we try some Sumo right here and right now according to the rules of the game. I could take ten of you all at the same time. If you think I'm lying, come on and give it a try. Surely you lot can see how it's supposed to be done?! Just attack like that. Come on, I'm only half your size. Let's have a Japanese Sumo bout!"

And with that, Maeda showed the men the basics of Sumo before dividing them into groups. As soon as the bouts started, the challengers found they had trouble resisting their natural inclination to drop down onto a knee or put a hand on the ground. So, the first two or three times Maeda fought each man when they pushed Maeda, he simply pulled them down with Hiki Otoshi, making them drop down onto one knee or he would redirect them so they would stumbling out of the circle. No matter how big they were Maeda was able to win easily. However, after five or six tries, they finally figured out this was not Judo, and the bouts became harder for Maeda to win. However, since he had beaten them soundly the first two or three times, the challengers began to nod with understanding.

Afterwards, Maeda said to them. "If I was able to defeat all of you like that, the Yokozuna Hitachiyama would be able to throw you all around like a rag doll. Japan is a country founded on martial arts. Thus it is its armed and unarmed combat methods are unparalleled the whole world over. You lot, on the other hand, focused solely on expanding your civilization, however, as you can see, when paired against this type of martial art, you are like a frog sitting at the bottom of a well, only aware of his small world."

Maeda continued, "So I think you all shouldn't be bragging about your art. It's unbelievable to me that you lot can look at the belly of a Japanese Sumo wrestler and joke that it looks like the belly of a pregnant woman. While it is certainly big and resembles the belly of a pregnant woman, a Sumo wrestler forges his body through years of rigorous training. When a Sumo wrestler puts power in his belly. You lot could put punch or head butt it as hard as you liked and not get the slightest reaction from him." The men hearing this all looked astounded.

If Hitachiyama had been in town when this occurred, Maeda could have given them the chance to face off against the grand champion Sumo wrestler, unfortunately Hitachi wasn't in London at that time. All around London, images of Japanese Sumo could be seen in color postcards or motion picture reels and this gave rise to heated discussions about which method of wrestling was better and which was worse. At these times Maeda would say, "If you lot were in Japan you would get beaten by any one of the innumerable Judo practitioners there. You would learn just how effective Sumo and Judo, the two types of Japanese wrestling, really are."

The following story is one Maeda heard later on from another friend:

When Hitachi was in New York he went to a certain athletic club in the city. A boxer at the gym laughed in scorn at the sight of the Japanese Sumo wrestler's fat belly. Hitachi got irritated by the man so he challenged the boxer, "Fella, you can hit me in the stomach as hard as you like, it won't make a dent in my belly. Go ahead and give it a try, punch me in the stomach!" And with that Hitachi stuck his belly out. The boxer retorted, "You are a big talker but when you get knocked unconscious you will be the laughingstock!" He then smirked and said, "Ok, I'm ready to take a punch at you!" With that he dropped into his stance, measured his breathing and threw a terrific punch. Hitachi had put power into his abdomen so the impact of the boxer's punch caused the attacker to rebound backwards one Ken, 182 cm/ 5'10." The Americans watching were astounded by the spectacle.

The Difference Between Eastern and Western Physical Education

Maeda's opinion is as follows:

"It is pretty clear that foreigners don't have any martial art that can stand up to Judo, however I would next like to see Japanese Sumo introduced overseas to it can be pitted against Western style wrestling and completely dominate it. With my Judo it is easy to defeat them, however the Western method of naked wrestling means that they are unable to handle a difference in weight between combatants. The only way to humble them is to defeat them in their own styles, namely the powerful Catch as catch can and Greco Roman styles of wrestling. Defeating them in this manner the only solution."

Maeda continues, "There is another problem with Western style wrestlers; if one is defeated by a wrestler from a different style, it is not considered a loss. This seems like more than enough evidence to classify the wrestling foreigners do as being a performance rather than a true art of self-defense. Thus, in order for Japanese Sumo wrestlers to become world champion wrestlers, they will have to learn western style wrestling and continue to train the various styles until they can challenge foreign wrestlers in their own style."

Maeda continues, "As for what are some good aspects of American and European styles of wrestling are, the answer is I love the rough intensity of the art. Sumo wrestlers like Hitachi and Umegaya[76] with their big bellies would have a hard time lasting thirty minutes or an hour after the bout has gone down to the ground."

One more aspect related to physical education that Maeda commented on were physical differences between Japanese and Westerners.

"After observing exercise coaches and wrestlers in America and Europe I noticed something about their bodies. The muscle development in Westerners is completely different from our country. When looking at foreigners you see beautifully developed muscles bulging out all over the body, on the other hand you don't see this

---

[76] Umegatani Totaro 梅ヶ谷藤太郎 (1845 ~ 1928) was the 15th Yokozuna.

too often in Japanese, whose bodies are naturally shaped without any outward bulges of muscle. Japanese bodies are smooth with the muscles pulled inside. Initially our bodies appear to be only fat without any bone or muscle however, when power is put into one part of the body, the well-developed muscles come bursting out. On the other hand, even at rest, the muscles in the bodies of foreigners appear to be rigid. When they put power into the muscles they don't become any harder. In short, they have no muscle flexibility. I think the muscle flexibility in Japanese is striking and is in fact superior. However I am not sure if this difference is due to the physical education method, an innate characteristic that makes Japanese a different race or even a difference that can be attributed to diet. I think this question should be researched scientifically."

Hitachiyama's Opinion on American and European Wrestling

Maeda and Hitachi talked about a great many things including Western wrestling and boxing. This is what Hitachi told Maeda,
"I will leave dealing with Western wrestlers up to you Judoka. As for boxing, we Sumo wrestlers will take them on!"

Maeda was puzzled by this statement, since he thought it would be the other way around and asked, "Why is that?"

In response Hitachi said, "It doesn't matter if a boxer hits a Sumo wrestler this way or that, such a blow won't even get a fart out of us! During regular training we crash into each other at full power, slamming our heads together. That is far more painful than taking a few hits."

Maeda couldn't disagree with that assessment. "I see, so tough Sumo wrestlers don't mind being the target of boxer's punches." Sumo wrestlers spend the whole year with their bellies out serving as training objects to younger members of the Sumo stable. Their faces are used to being slapped and struck and their hands are used shoving. If a Sumo wrestler took on a top level boxer, it is not at all clear who would emerge the winner." Maeda stared off into the distance and spoke what was in his heart, "I wonder if there is some Japanese Sumo wrestler who would be willing to take on the black boxer Johnson who toppled Jeffries and be crowned with a laurel wreath as world champion!"

No doubt there are some people wondering why Maeda didn't

challenge Johnson to a fight. The truth was, if someone asked him to battle Johnson, he would do so at the drop of a hat. He was by no means certain he would win, however he was not the least afraid. Since his body was small, he couldn't fight like Hitachi and let his body serve as a target for his opponent, entrusting that the blows would rebound off his body. If the fight was actually going to take place, Maeda simply had to mentally accept that he may well get beat to a pulp. So pretty easy overall.

However, Westerners would not have an easy time learning another style of fighting. A boxer would likely be fearful going into a Judo match with a Judoka. If a Japanese person was going to challenge a boxer, he would have to learn that style of fighting as well as all the rules. The term "world champion" gets thrown around a lot in the West, however placing Japan outside the "world" is an error. Someone like Tamatsubaki[77] could cross the bridge from the Sumo capital Ryogoku over to the boxing realm. While his big belly would be in the way, if he trained in boxing he would be able to take on Johnson despite the other side, the one that always says "different weights are not fair, different schools are not fair" being unable to even reach the Komusubi level of Sumo.[78] So is there anyone who has what it takes to take on and overthrow Johnson thereby becoming world champion? Someone with the will to do this would have the chance to really turn the tables.

The muscles of Japanese Sumo wrestlers are soft and flexible that is why people try to scoff and say it's all fat. Maeda has an interesting story about that:

One day he was invited to a certain pub and he and Hitachi set off together. When they arrived the pair were treated to whiskey and other sorts of fragrant alcohol. Eventually the topic of conversation

---

[77] Tamatsubaki Kentarō 玉椿憲太郎 (1883 ~ 1928) Though only 158 cm/5 ft 2 in, 73 kg (161 lb)he gave the likes of Hitachiyama and others a real challenge and was called the "mite He was the shortest wrestler in sumo history,[2] and also one of the lightest at 73 kg. a
[78] This is the fourth highest rank in Sumo wrestling and is the lowest of the so-called titleholder ranks, or San-yaku. Thus Maeda is casting doubt as to whether Westerners could become skilled enough in Sumo to advance to the upper echelons.

turned to Japanese Sumo. The westerners, including the wives of high-ranking officials, seeing Hitachi's fat, blubbery body reckoned there was no way he could actually wrestle. Hitachi laughed, "If you think this is all blubber, I will take off my pants and show you!" Maeda was hesitant to encourage Hitachi as there were high-class ladies present however Hitachi plowed on like an avalanche. "The ladies present will no doubt say that they think it would be untoward, however deep in their hearts they want to take a look at a man's skin!" Hitachi followed up that rude comment with, "Well then, this may be a bit rude but anyone who wants to look can see that my body is not just blubbering fat!"

Everyone in the group began shouting they wanted to see. Hitachi declared boldly, "I don't care what anyone thinks, the legs of a Yokozuna grand champion are a marvel to behold!" And, with a few more self-aggrandizing statements he rolled up his pants and exposed his statuesque legs in a scene that commanded everyone's attention. The ladies in the group all began touching his legs with their quick slender hands all while saying, "Me too! Me too! I want to touch!" They were all astounded at how the muscles in his legs felt like stone.

If Hitachi had appeared in Japanese dress and then stripped down to just his loin cloth and done the Dohyo Iri it would have brought down the house.

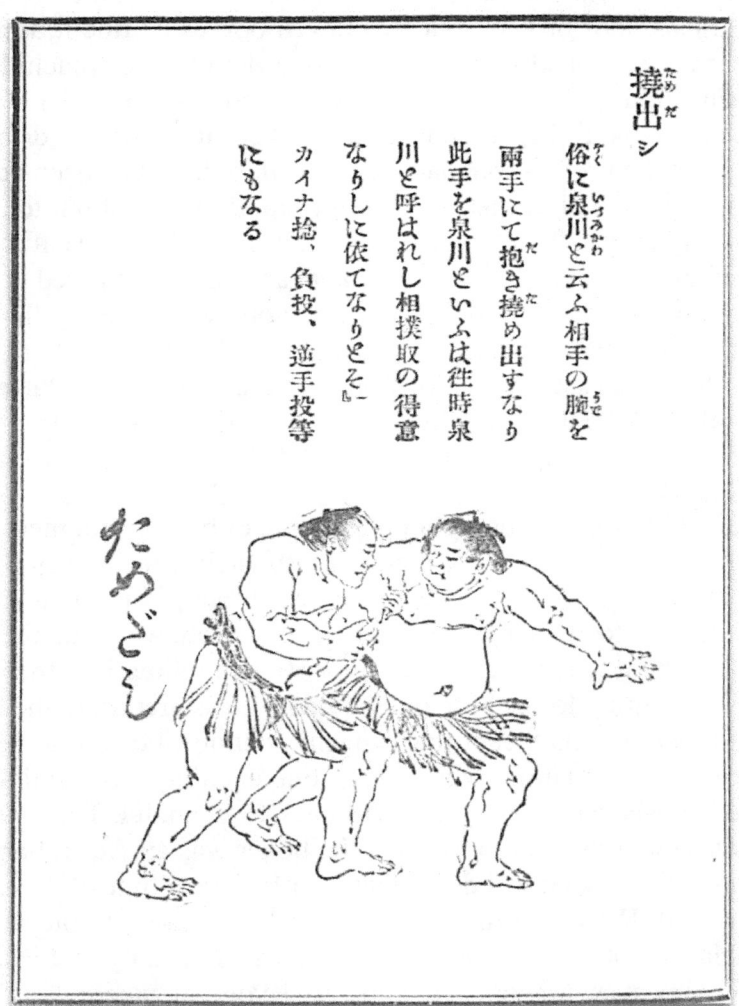

The Sumo technique Izumikawa, also known as Tame Dashi. The technique involves using both arms to wrap up one of your opponent's arms and then force him out of the ring. "Izumikawa" is said to be a Sumo wrestler who was an expert at this technique.

Illustrated Guide to the Forty-Eight Sumo Techniques
図解奥伝相撲四十八手
Hankei Sanshi 半渓散史 1918

One night Hitachi was invited to ambassador Komura's[79] house. The ambassador brought out two dozen bottles of fine Masamune Sake, that was usually served to visiting dignitaries. Hitachi began drinking along with Maeda and the other Judoka in attendance, who were all ranked Maku-uchi-level[80] when it came to drinking. Therefore the group soon made short work of the two dozen bottles. Following the end of that bout, the group as one went out to attack Piccadilly circus. They swept legs and broke balance, went in with the left arm attacking with Izumikawa, and the battle raged hot and heavy until legs were wobbly and everyone was swaying this way and that. They made a stand at the edge of the Dohyo, right by the rope, holding fast and glaring all around with eyes blurred by alcohol.[81] And before long the group realized that the electric lamps that lit Piccadilly circus were out and they had faint shadows now as night gave way to dawn.

Hitachi frequently brought up the topic of boxing and mentioned that he would like to see a match. Fortunately Maeda was friends with the manager of the London National Boxing Club and one night they all went to see some matches. As they were watching the third or fourth bout, a messenger came for Hitachi telling him there was a person waiting to see him and would he please return to the hotel. Unfortunately, this meant that Hitachi wouldn't be able to see the end of the bout. Things were just getting exciting but it couldn't be helped so Maeda and Hitachi went back to the hotel. The next day Maeda saw in the newspaper that the boxer was an Australian man "small soldier" who had defended his title fifteen times.[82]

All told, Hitachi spent two weeks in London and throughout he and Maeda got along famously. The pair had actually met in Japan a few times as Maeda had gone to Ryogoku where the Sumo

---

[79] Komura Jutaro 小村壽太郎 (1855~1911.)

[80] Makuuchi 幕内, or makunouchi 幕の内, is the top division of the six divisions of professional Sumo.

[81] 醉眼朦朧 one's eyes blurred from drinking; with drunken eyes; dazed by wine

[82] Possibly referring to Albert Griffiths (1871~1927), better known as Young Griffo, was a World Featherweight boxing champion from 1890 to 1892.

matches are held, to train several times. However, their conversations had never gone past greetings. Now that Maeda had a chance to talk with the Sumo champion, he found the giant man's gregarious manner appealing, especially when he unabashedly praised himself. He would declare boastfully, "That's true, I am great!" Truly a man with a lot of self-confidence. Before Hitachi departed London, he bought himself a set of boxing gear.

So after Hitachi travelled from London to Paris, Maeda found he was a bit lonely. It felt quiet like after a big windstorm had abated and suddenly Maeda had had enough of London. He decided to set off for Belgium.

Maeda felt that there were other Judoka who had been in London teaching Judo for years before Maeda arrived, Maeda now felt he would like to develop the art in a new land. While he would have rather headed to a larger county, he was going to have to pay his own way so Belgium was an inexpensive option. If he were offered an invitation to a larger country he would of course accept, however barring that, paying the expensive travel fees and daily expenses to go to a country that he couldn't speak the language of while trying to spread Judo would be quite difficult. Thus, he could zip over to Belgium and if things didn't go well he could always return to London which was close by and therefore an easy trip.

So, he went about making preparations for a two week stay in Belgium.

www.ingramcontent.com/pod-product-compliance
Lightning Source LLC
Chambersburg PA
CBHW050634160426
43194CB00010B/1670